ABOUT T

Barbara Cartland, the wo
novelist, who is also an hi
political speaker and television personality, has now written
over 490 books and sold nearly 500 million copies all over
the world.

She has also had many historical works published and
has written four autobiographies as well as the biographies
of her mother and that of her brother, Ronald Cartland,
who was the first Member of Parliament to be killed in
the last war. This book has a preface by Sir Winston
Churchill and has just been republished with an
introduction by the late Sir Arthur Bryant.

"Love at the Helm" a novel written with the help and
inspiration of the late Earl Mountbatten of Burma, Great
Uncle of His Royal Highness The Price of Wales, is being
sold for the Mountbatten Memorial Trust.

She has broken the world record for the last thirteen
years by writing an average of twenty-three books a year.
In the Guinness Book of Records she is listed as the world's
top-selling author.

Miss Cartland in 1978 sang an Album of Love Songs
with the Royal Philharmonic Orchestra.

In private life Barbara Cartland, who is a Dame of Grace
of the Order of St. John of Jerusalem, Chairman of the
St. John Council in Hertfordshire and Deputy President
of the St. John Ambulance Brigade, has fought for better
conditions and salaries for Midwives and Nurses.

She championed the cause for the Elderly in 1956
invoking a Government Enquiry into the "Housing
Conditions of Old People".

In 1962 she had the Law of England changed so that
Local Authorities had to provide camps for their own
Gypsies. This has meant that since then thousands and
thousands of Gypsy children have been able to go to School
which they had never been able to do in the past, as their

caravans were moved every twenty-four hours by the Police.

There are now fourteen camps in Hertfordshire and Barbara Cartland has her own Romany Gypsy, Camp called Barbaraville by the Gypsies.

Her designs "Decorating with Love" are being sold all over the U.S.A. and the National Home Fashions League made her, in 1981, "Woman of Achievement".

Barbara Cartland's book "Getting Older, Growing Younger" has been published in Great Britain and the U.S.A. and her fifth Cookery Book, "The Romance of Food", is now being used by the House of Commons.

In 1984 she received at Kennedy Airport, America's Bishop Wright Air Industry Award for her contribution to the development of aviation. In 1931 she and two R.A.F. Officers thought of, and carried the first aeroplane-towed glider air-mail.

During the War she was Chief Lady Welfare Officer in Bedfordshire looking after 20,000 Service men and women. She thought of having a pool of Wedding Dresses at the War Office so a Service Bride could hire a gown for the day.

She bought second hand 1,000 gowns without coupons for the A.T.S., the W.A.A.F.s and the W.R.E.N.S. In 1945 Barbara Cartland received the Certificate of Merit from Eastern Command.

In 1964 Barbara Cartland founded the National Association for Health of which she is the President, as a front for all the Health Stores and for any product made as alternative medicine.

This has now a £500,000,000 turnover a year, with one third going in export.

In January 1988 she received "La Medaille de Vermeil de la Ville de Paris", (the Gold Medal of Paris). This is the highest award to be given by the City of Paris for ACHIEVEMENT — 25 million books sold in France.

In March 1988 Barbara Cartland was asked by the Prime

Minister of India Rajid Gandhi and the Indian Government to open their Health Resort outside Delhi. This is almost the largest Health Resort in the world.

Barbara Cartland was received with great enthusiasm by her fans, who also fêted her at a Reception in the city and she received the gift of an embossed plate from the Government.

OTHER BOOKS BY BARBARA CARTLAND

Romantic Novels, over 490 the most recently published being:

Hidden by Love	The Dangerous Marriage
Walking to Wonderland	Good or Bad
Lucky Logan Finds Love	This is Love
Born of Love	Seek the Stars
The Angel and the Rake	Escape to Love
The Queen of Hearts	Look with the Heart
The Wicked Widow	Safe in Paradise
To Scotland and Love	Love in the Ruins
Love and War	Coronation of Love
Love at the Ritz	A Duel of Jewels

The Dream and the Glory (In aid of the St. John Ambulance Brigade)

Autobiographical and Biographical:

The Isthmus Years	1919-1939
The Years of Opportunity	1939-1945
I Search for Rainbows	1945-1976
We Danced All Night	1919-1929

Ronald Cartland (With a foreword by Sir Winston Churchill)
Polly — My Wonderful Mother
I Seek the Miraculous

Historical:

Bewitching Women
The Outrageous Queen (The Story of Queen Christina of Sweden)
The Scandalous Life of King Carol
The Private Life of Charles II
The Private Life of Elizabeth, Empress of Austria
Josephine, Empress of France
Diane de Poitiers
Metternich – The Passionate Diplomat
A Year of Royal Days

Sociology:

You in the Home
The Fascinating Forties
Marriage for Moderns
Be Vivid, Be Vital
Love, Life and Sex
Vitamins for Vitality
Husbands and Wives
Men and Wonderful
Woman the Enigma
Etiquette
The Many Facets of Love
Sex and the Teenager
The Book of Charm
Living Together
The Youth Secret
The Magic of Honey
The Book of Beauty and Health

Keep Young and Beautiful by Barbara Cartland and Elinor Glyn
Etiquette for Love and Romance
Barbara Cartland's Book of Health

Cookery:

Barbara Cartland's Health Food Cookery Book
Food for Love
Magic of Honey Cookbook
Recipes for Lovers
The Romance of Food

Editor of:

"The Common Problem" by Ronald Cartland (with a preface by the Rt. Hon. the Earl of Selborne, P.C.)

Barbara Cartland's Library of Love
                                    Library of Ancient Wisdom

"Written with Love" Passionate love letters selected by Barbara Cartland

Drama:

Blood Money
French Dressing

Philosophy:

Touch the Stars

Radio Operetta:

The Rose and the Violet (Music by Mark Lubbock) Performed in 1942.

Radio Plays:

The Caged Bird: An episode in the life of Elizabeth Empress of Austria Performed in 1957.

General:

Barbara Cartland's Book of Useless Information with a Foreword by the Earl Mountbatten of Burma.
(In aid of the United World Colleges)

Love and Lovers   (Picture Book)

The Light of Love   (Prayer Book)

Barbara Cartland's Scrapbook
(In aid of the Royal Photographic Museum)

Romantic Royal Marriages

Barbara Cartland's Book of Celebrities

Getting Older, Growing Younger

Verse:

Lines on Life and Love

Music:

An Album of Love Songs sung with the Royal Philharmonic Orchestra.

Films:

The Flame is Love
A Hazard of Hearts
The Lady and The Highwayman

Cartoons:

Barbara Cartland Romances (Book of Cartoons) has recently been published in the U.S.A., Great Britain, and other parts of the world.

Children:

A Children's Pop-Up Book: "Princess to the Rescue"

Videos:

A Hazard of Hearts
The Lady and The Highwayman

"ROYAL JEWELS"

BY

BARBARA CARTLAND

This book required an enormous
amount of research and I am
deeply grateful for the untiring
help of Audrey Elliott,
Hazel Clark, and Sally Barnes.

Drawings by Trefor Salter.

"ROYAL JEWELLERY"

ISBN 0 905377 45 1

First Publication in Great Britain

Copyright © 1989 Cartland Promotions

Published by
Marwain Publishing Limited
Marwain House
Clarke Road
Mount Farm
Milton Keynes
MK1 1LG

Typeset by
Grillford Limited, Granby, Milton Keynes

Printed and bound by
Richard Clay, Bungay, Suffolk

CONTENTS

QUEEN VICTORIA
1819-1901

When the eighteen-year-old Princess Victoria of Kent acceded to the throne of England, in her inheritance was a priceless collection of jewels, which included the pearls bought by Queen Elizabeth and diamonds that had belonged to King George III.

During his reign King William IV used stones from a number of old pieces in the Royal coffers to create fashionable new jewels which were worn by his wife Queen Adelaide.

When he died in 1837 she handed them on to her much loved niece, Queen Victoria.

Unfortunately, due to a dispute in the family, Queen Victoria was denied the right to many of the jewels she had been given.

In all started in 1714 when the Stuart line ended with the death of Queen Anne.

She was succeeded by her second cousin the Elector of Hanover — King George I.

Until 1837 the British Kings ruled both Britain and Hanover. King George I and King George II each had divided their time between the two countries and were careful to keep the heirlooms of their two inheritances separate.

When King George II died in 1760 he left half his personal collection of jewels to his grandson and heir, King George III, and the other half to his surviving son, William Augustus, Duke of Cumberland.

In 1761 the Duke sold his share for £50,000 to King George III, who gave the jewels to his bride, Princess Charlotte of Mecklenburg-Strelitz, as a wedding gift.

Queen Charlotte stored these jewels separately from the rest she owned and on her death in 1818 left them to 'The House of Hanover'.

Then came the cause of the dispute.

In 1833 the Kingdom of Hanover passed new Salic laws conforming to the Germanic code that excluded women from the succession as long as any male members of the family survived.

That was why when King George II's son King William IV died in 1837 his successor, Queen Victoria, could not succeed to the throne of Hanover and the two Kingdoms were separated for the first time in 123 years.

Ernest Augustus, Duke of Cumberland, became King of Hanover.

He immediately demanded a portion of the jewels left by King William as part of his inheritance, both as King of Hanover and as a son of Queen Charlotte.

Queen Victoria refused arguing that whatever jewels she possessed had been purchased with English money.

She insisted on wearing the disputed pieces, not just because she felt she had the right, but also because she had few other pieces of her own.

King Ernest wrote a letter to a friend in which he said sarcastically:

"I hear the little Queen is loaded with my diamonds, which made a very fine show."

The wrangling continued until twenty years after the dispute started, it found favour in Hanover.

Delivered into the hands of the Hanoverian Ambassador, Count Kielmansegge on 28th January 1858 were jewels which included Queen Charlotte's diamond wedding crown, diamond stomacher, and a diamond necklace and cross.

During the sixty-four years of Queen Victoria's reign her collection of jewels probably increased ten-fold.

Queen Victoria's husband was extremely artistic and designed a number of pieces for her.

She received jewellery as gifts from her ever expanding Empire.

Despite the magnificence of her diamonds, sapphires,

rubies, pearls and opals, the Queen was just as happy wearing trinkets with a sentimental value attached to them.

Among the first of these keepsakes was a bracelet with her fiance's portrait as its centrepiece and this she wore when she announced on 23rd November 1839 her impending marriage to Prince Albert of Saxe-Coburg-Gotha.

She later told Lord Melbourne, the Prime Minister, that Prince Albert's portrait had given her the courage to face the eighty-two members of her Privy Council.

Prince Albert later gave her a pair of bracelets on which were mounted miniatures of their nine children.

One of the Queen's most treasured possessions in her old age was a brooch of diamonds and pearls which was given to her on the occasion of her Jubilee by the members of her household.

They were delighted to see her wearing it at the dinner to mark the Jubilee.

QUEEN VICTORIA

QUEEN CLEOPATRA OF EGYPT
69-30 B.C.

Queen Cleopatra was the sixth Queen of Egypt by that name.

On the death of her father she became joint Sovereign with her brother Ptolemy XII, who she married in accordance with Egyptian custom.

When the Romans invaded Egypt the Roman General, Julius Caesar, became Governor.

Cleopatra seduced him by being carried into his presence and rolled out of a carpet at his feet.

She was 21 years of age, exceedingly beautiful, not Egyptian, but Macedonian.

Her skin was as white as milk, her eyes as blue as the Aegean, her hair was burnished gold.

Caesar looked, loved and was conquered.

Two years later he was recalled to Rome where he was offered the Crown.

Mark Antony, a celebrated Roman General was sent to Egypt in his place.

When Queen Cleopatra heard that he was coming she sailed down the Nile to Alexandria in a ship glittering with gold from stem to stern.

The sails were of purple silk, silver oars dipped rhythmically to the sound of music.

The barge glittered and glimmered with constellations of lights like great branches of clustered grapes.

Jade-green and purple lights swung from the masts.

Lights shone upwards from chalices of lilies and some shone from the hearts of roses.

They wreathed the ship and on the poop shone a golden canopy starred with light.

On an altar of beauty lay the Queen.

Bare-bosomed, she was girt about the waist with a girdle of great rubies, flashing fire as she breathed.

On her head was the golden crown of Venus and in one

hand she held the goddess's own sceptre — a thornless bough of roses.

As Mark Antony stepped aboard, great veils with silver peacocks and peonies fell from the masts hiding their meeting from the crowd of onlookers who clustered on the Quay.

The music ceased as he reached the Queen's mysterious golden couch.

She raised herself on one elbow and extended her swan-white hand.

"At last!" she said with a little sigh like the pleasure of a child, and fell back on the rosy pillows.

Caesar at 55, had been an old, somewhat restrained man.

Mark Antony was 42, exceedingly strong, experienced and ardent in love, masculine and virile. Cleopatra fell passionately in love with him.

They loved, laughed and were wildly happy.

What was Rome and its feeble efforts to Alexandria, the abode of the Gods and Pharaohs?

What could compare with being with the most beautiful woman in the world?

One evening, Mark Antony watched as a cup was set before Cleopatra containing vinegar.

He wondered if it was a charm or some magic she had not used before.

In Cleopatra's little ears swung two enormous pearls, the shell-pink lights playing on their milky beauty.

She took one of these and laid it in the vinegar, a smile at the corners of her exquisite lips, while Mark Antony watched spell-bound.

She was stirring it slowly with the stem of a rose which lay beneath her.

When the pearl had dissolved she held out the cup towards him.

He took it from her and lifted it saying:

"To you, my beautiful beloved little Goddess. Good health!"

As he drank he realised she had given him the most expensive aphrodisiac the world had ever known.

Pearls were the oldest and most treasured of jewels and supremely valuable.

As Mark Antony knew, the Roman General Vitellius had paid for an entire campaign by selling one of his mother's earrings which was not nearly as fine as Cleopatra's.

Whether it was due to the pearl or not, they were exceedingly happy.

They rode and hunted furiously on the verge of the desert; the Queen riding astride like a boy.

She was fearless and reckless until Mark Antony was nervous for the exquisite, light figure dashing ahead, and all that it meant to him.

They had picnic parties on smooth seas, drifting between blue sky and bluer ocean.

In the background there was the sound of lutes and flutes, so sweet that it seemed as if the gods themselves were afloat with them.

There were delightful fishing scenes, when they and members of their Court vied with each other with green rods.

They were all lucky but Antony did not shine as an Angler.

There was one unforgettable day when, piqued by those who laughed at him, Antony made an Egyptian boy dive and swim snakelike under the water to impale an enormous fish upon his hook.

Antony thought he had deceived Cleopatra, but she saw everything and with a finger to her lips told the others to pretend they thought he had been successful.

Antony began to believe that the Queen's love would make this Paradise his own for ever.

She possessed him utterly and for the first time he was aware of the passion that was not only sensuous, but came from the deeper sources of his mind and heart.

In the past, it had always been easy for him to love and run away.

Now everything was changed.

She enchanted him and at the same time he was terrified.

Terrified because although he possessed her body, she never surrendered completely.

Even when he made love to her in a way that should have made her the other half of him, she was always herself.

Not his, as not completely and absolutely would she surrender.

She gave him twins, a boy and a girl, both beautiful and adorable.

And yet she was still in some strange, inimitable way, spiritually, if not physically out of reach.

The tragedy of their lives lay ahead, but still for Antony, there were no clouds on the sunlit horizon.

. . . .

The Peregrina Pearl is probably the most famous in the world.

It has always been believed that it is the sister of the pearl which Queen Cleopatra dissolved in vinegar as an aphrodisiac.

It was found in the Gulf of Panama by a black slave who won his freedom as a result.

Philip II of Spain acquired it and gave it to his wife, Mary Tudor, Queen of England. On her death the pearl went back to Spain.

From then it was worn by a succession of Kings and Queens of that country.

When Napoleon's brother Joseph escaped from Spain after the battle of Waterloo, he took with him in his pocket the Peregrina Pearl, and left it to his nephew Prince Louis Napoleon, III.

When Prince Louis came to London in Exile, he brought La Peregrina with him and sold it to the Duke of Abercorn with whom he was a close friend.

The Duchess often wore it but the Pearl had never been

bored and it was so heavy that it was constantly falling from its setting. She lost it three times. Once at a Ball at Buckingham Palace, she found that the great Pearl had gone from her neck and was frantic to find it.

On going into Supper she saw La Peregrina gleaming at her from the folds of a velvet train of the Lady immediately in front of her.

The Peregrina Pearl remained with the family until 1968 when the Duke sold it to the film-star Richard Burton who gave it to Elizabeth Taylor.

QUEEN CLEOPATRA OF EGYPT

THE EMPEROR CHARLEMAGNE
(Charles the Great)
743-814

The Emperor Charlemagne, who was also known as Charles the Great, was King of the Franks from 768 to 814 and Emperor from 800 to 814.

He was one of the greatest and most brilliant Kings there has ever been.

He and his brother divided all the territory stretching in a vast arc around them and they determined to make the peoples in each Kingdom embrace Christianity.

They were violently opposed, but King Charlemagne was an exceedingly experienced and intelligent soldier.

He conducted his campaigns with amazing efficiency taking two Armies into Italy; one through the Great St. Bernard, the other through the Mont Cenis pass.

He planned campaigns North and South of the Alps subduing rebellion after rebellion against him.

He established North/Western coasts of his Kingdom against the Vikings of Denmark in the 9th century and succeeded in exacting permanent recognition from the Bretons.

As a Ruler of so vast a group of territories, Charlemagne was indisputably the Arbiter of the West.

In fact, the Church itself, in Western Europe, looked for leadership to the Frankish King.

When visiting Rome, The Emperor changed his Frankish clothes and put on a Roman tunic, to enter St. Peter's. He must have marvelled at the wonderful building of the Emperor Constantine the Great, and knelt at the High Altar in his devotions.

A little while later the Pope crept up behind him, and without being heard jammed on his head a crown.

The audience who had been watching the episode roared with laughter and called out:

"To Charles August, crowned by God, Great and

21

Peaceful Emperor of the Romans, long life and victory
. . ."

Charlemagne made a great show of surprise, and swore that he had been made Emperor without his knowledge or consent.

When the Emperor was too old to go on fighting, he fell in love with a woman of inferior rank.

She used magic to hold the King's affections and when she died the Emperor was too grief-stricken to accept the fact.

He had her body embalmed and placed in his bed.

The Bishop of Cologne, the King's confessor, was worried by his Emperor's obsession.

He prayed for help and was instructed by a heavenly voice to open the mouth of the corpse.

He did so and removed from under the tongue a ring decorated with two sapphires and a fragment of the Holy Cross.

As soon as the magic token was removed the Emperor hastily had the woman's body buried.

He then however demanded the constant companionship of the Bishop.

This became an embarrassment, especially as the King had made him Archbishop of Mainz and Chancellor of the Holy Roman Empire.

In desperation to get on with his duties, he threw the ring into the lake which was in the middle of a marsh.

From that moment the Emperor was no longer interested in any human company, but built a house by the lake where he lived until his death.

Yet even as he lay dying and in pain, the magic of the ring still held him to life on earth.

He was however, in such agony that the Archbishop dragged the lake for the ring and carried it to the dying Emperor.

As he held it in his hand Emperor Charlemagne quietly died.

In the year 1000, Emperor Otto III had Charlemagne's

tomb at Aix-la-Chapelle opened.

The great Charlemagne was found sitting on a marble throne, perfectly preserved, his legendary white beard stretched across his chest.

Otto removed from his neck a talisman.

Set in gold were two cabochon sapphires and a relic of the Holy Cross.

This remained in the Treasure House until 1804, when the Chapter of the Cathedral presented it to Empress Josephine for her coronation with Napoleon Bonaparte.

Eventually it was inherited by the Empress Eugénie, wife of Napoleon III.

After the fall of the Second Empire in 1870 she took it with her into exile in England.

When the Germans bombed the Cathedral of Reims in the First World War, the former Empress, horrified by such an act of vandalism, returned the Talisman of Charlemagne to the Cathedral, where it remains to this day.

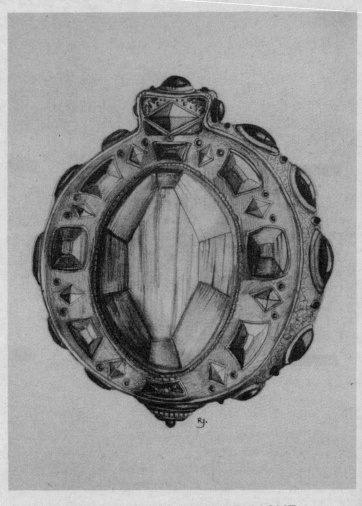

THE EMPEROR CHARLEMAGNE

24

EMPEROR NAPOLEON BONAPARTE
1769-1821

Napoleon was born at Ajaccio in Corsica.

He was sent to France to receive a Military education and was a Captain at the age of twenty.

In 1794 he served in Italy with such distinction that he won a Generalship, and the next year was appointed Commander-in-Chief.

A series of most brilliant successes followed.

He defeated the Austrian forces in 1797, conducted an expedition to Syria and Egypt in 1798, returned in 1799 to find himself the most popular man in France.

In November of that year he proclaimed himself First Consul.

In 1800 he was again in Italy and once more victorious.

In 1804 he was made Emperor, and had what is known as 'The Regent Diamond' placed in the hilt of his Coronation sword.

This diamond is one of the purest and brightest in the world.

In 1701 a slave working in the Paretial Mines in India found the stone and in order to escape with it, he deliberately injured himself in the thigh.

He then hid the stone under the bandage.

In return for the diamond a sailor promised to help the slave to flee, but murdered him instead, and tossed the body overboard.

The gem passed through the hands of the Governor of the Fortress of St. George, Thomas Pitt, the grandfather of William Pitt Earl of Chatham when he was Governor of Madras, and the Duke of Orleans Regent of France.

He was ready to pay any price for an alliance with England and paid two-and-a-half million pounds for the gem, which was for ever afterwards known as the Regent.

The Regent disappeared with the other diamonds of the Crown in the robbery of 1792 and later was found hidden behind a beam in an attic in Paris.

In 1805 Napoleon was in the field against England, Russia and Austria.

He achieved a splendid series of victories at Austerlitz and elsewhere.

He practically became Dictator of Europe and distributed Kingships amongt his brothers in the most profuse manner.

Joseph became King of Naples, Louis King of Holland and Jerome King of Westphalia.

His invasion of Russia was however disastrous, the Peninsula War went against him.

In 1814 the Allies entered Paris and forced him to abdicate.

Napoleon's second wife, the Empress Marie Louise escaped from the Capital with the Crown Jewels.

She was in constant danger of being stopped and searched, or robbed by marauding Cossacks.

The Coronation Sword with the Regent Diamond was too long to hide under her clothes with the other jewels.

One of her faithful Courtiers, *Monsieur* de Meneval, broke the sword and hid the hilt under his coat.

Cossacks eventually did stop the carriage, but they found no jewels, since they dared not search the august personages inside.

By order of Napoleon the Regent was returned to the provisional government and reinstated in the treasures of the Crown.

When the Second Empire fell in 1870, the triumphant Commune sent representatives to the Bank of France with orders to hand over the Crown Jewels, including the Regent.

However, the Communards' threats of violence met with no success.

Shortly before the Empire crumbled, the diamonds, and the Regent had been removed in an iron box marked *'SPECIAL PROJECTILES'* and sent from Paris to Brest.

There it stayed on a ship, ready to sail if the situation grew worse.

The Commune was crushed in May 1871, and the Regent went back to the Louvre.

Napoleon was sent to Elba, but made his escape and gathered his old Army about him.

They went forth to meet the English and Prussian Armies.

He was finally completely defeated at Waterloo on the 18th June 1815, and exiled to St. Helena, where he died six years later.

His remains were removed to Paris in 1840 where they rest in a magnificent tomb.

NAPOLEON BONAPARTE

MATILDA OF FLANDERS – QUEEN OF ENGLAND
1031-1083

Matilda was the daughter of the Earl of Flanders.

She was very beautiful and counted among her ancestors the highly born French as well as the English, German and Norman blood.

She was well-educated but very small of stature, although exceedingly graceful. She was 4 ft. 2 ins. high, the only Queen of England who was a dwarf.

As soon as Duke William of Normandy saw her he began to woo her, but her father was not pleased.

The Earl of Flanders had no wish for his extremely well-connected daughter to be married to Duke William, who was a bastard and whose claim to the Kingdom of Normandy was somewhat dubious.

Moreover, they were Cousins and the Church disapproved of congenerous marriages.

As it happened, Matilda had already fallen in love with a young Englishman who had come to her father's Court on a Diplomatic mission.

However, Duke William was a man who liked to have his own way and as his peaceful approaches to Matilda failed, he resorted to violence.

One morning, as Matilda emerged from Church he sprang at her, tore her clothing, dragged her down in the street and gave her several slaps.

He did not abduct her, but rode away.

At this time she was only sixteen years old and he was twenty.

Although the Earl of Flanders was not impressed by Duke William's antecedents, he was descended from his great-grandfather, Duke Rollo of Normandy.

Among the descendants of Duke Rollo, especially through the Granville line are many of the great families of Britain – Landsdowne, Bath, Sutherland, Dysent and the Earl Spencer.

Duke William was also related through Duke Rollo to three English Kings — Ethelred the Unready, Edward the Confessor and King Canute.

Matilda, not pleased at William's behaviour refused to consider marrying him, but William had no intention of giving up.

At the same time she could not help being thrilled that he was so masterful and, like many women, she wanted to be conquered.

Eventually, she accepted him, but they waited five years before the actual marriage ceremony took place, in 1053.

The Earl had changed his mind and he gave Matilda to William joyfully.

The Duke William's position had improved, but he still had many enemies, some within his own Dukedom.

The Pope showed his displeasure at this marriage by excommunicating them both.

Then His Holiness relented on condition that they erect a religious house.

Duke William built St. Stephen's Abbey for Monks — Matilda Abbaye-Aux-Dames at Cannes for Nuns.

In the meantime, their marriage was extremely happy, Matilda was deeply in love with William and he with her.

Because a woman can always make a man do great deeds if he loves her enough, he was determined to conquer England.

William had already proved himself as being an extremely experienced Ruler, administrator and commander.

His own Duchy was outstanding.

He, however, was determined to go further afield.

William set out on his great enterprise — the conquest of England.

He left his wife in charge of Normandy.

In return for his gesture of confidence, Matilda had built and fitted out a secret ship to add to William's gathering Fleet.

She spared no expense; the figurehead was of gold, an effigy of their youngest son, holding in one hand a bow, its arrow aimed towards England, in the other a trumpet.

William made it his flagship.

He embarked for England in boats which might easily have capsized as they crossed the Channel.

When he won the Battle of Hastings he had three horses killed under him.

With the Saxons defeated, he proclaimed himself King of All England and decided to be crowned at Westminster Abbey.

He showed the Anglo-Saxon nobles how a King should live.

At Christmas and Whitsun he put on a calculated display of magnificence and all the delicacies of food from Constantinople, Babylon, Tripoli, Syria and Phoenicia.

The Norman Courts set new standards of social behaviour and a new elegance.

Matilda first set foot in England in April, 1068, and on Whit-Sunday of that year William, who had been crowned already, shared her Coronation in order to make the occasion more splendid.

She was the first real Queen of England.

Her crown, which unfortunately did not survive, was a beautiful shape and of diamonds set with large capusson emeralds.

William was exceedingly clever in his conquest of England. Except when faced with utter defiance, he followed a policy of consideration.

Matilda gave William four sons and several daughters.

It was due to her influence that William made laws for keeping Law and Order. One said:

'If a man lay with a woman against her will he is forthwith condemned to forfeit those members with which he desported himself.'

William was entirely faithful to Matilda, which was very unusual in those days.

He trusted her implicitly and allowed her to share all

his glories.

Matilda died in Normandy when she was fifty-one and William, who was in England, hastened to her bedside.

They had loved each other devotedly and he told her as she lay dying that there had never been any other woman in his heart and never would be.

"I love you, I love you!" he swore, "and life will never be the same if you leave me."

She had, in fact, been his talisman.

After her death he was so grieved that, much as he loved hunting, he gave it up.

In the four years of his widowhood his luck seemed to desert him and he died in great pain 'without a friend or kinsman near his bed'.

His last prayer was:

"I commend myself to Mary the Holy Mother of God, my Heavenly Mistress, that by her Blessed intercession, I may be reconciled to her Beloved Son, Our Lord Jesus Christ."

After that he died instantly.

MATILDA OF FLANDERS

SHAH JEHAN

SHAH JEHAN
d. 1666

It was Shah Jehan, son and successor of Jehangir who bankrupted his Empire by building the immortal monuments of the Mogul age.

Shah Jehan, who loved jewels, usually wore four-million-pounds worth and stored those estimated now at six-million pounds.

The Hall of private audience in the Red Fort at Delhi had walls of precious stones bedded in marble, a ceiling of beaten silver and a Peacock throne of solid gold.

Above the throne was a tree made of gold, from which hung fruit comprised of diamonds and rubies. On either side the Peacocks which were of gold, had their spread tails studded with emeralds and sapphires.

The Pearl Mosque at Agra sent the spirit soaring in rapture.

The Shalimar Gardens in Kashmir were a dream of delight.

When Shah Jehan's beloved Mumtaz Mahal died, aged thirty-nine, after the birth of their fourteenth child, he was broken-hearted. He set 20,000 men to work on her tomb and when the Taj Mahal (a play on her name) was finished it was, and still is, one of the Wonders of the World.

No woman has ever had a more exquisite memorial erected to commemorate a great and enduring love. To see it lifts the heart with the ecstasy which only love can bring.

The Koh-i-Noor Diamond was set in the Peacock throne of the Shah.

It is believed to have originated from Golconda in India and its history has been traced back to when it was part of the treasure of the Rajahs of Malwa.

In 1739 it fell into the hands of Nadir Shah at the sack of Delhi and it was he who is thought to have given the stone its name 'Koh-i-Noor', meaning 'Mountain of Light'.

When it was presented to Queen Victoria, she was disappointed because she thought it did not sparkle, and she had it recut to show more fire.

The Koh-i-Noor adorns the crown of the Queen Consort because it has the reputation of bringing bad luck to men, but good fortune to women.

Its original weight of 191 carats was reduced to 108.3 carats after recutting.

It is now on display in the Tower of London.

ALFRED THE GREAT, KING OF WESSEX
849-899

After a long and terrible battle against the Danes in 878, King Alfred was forced to hide in the marshes of Somerset.

It was believed that there he lost a talisman of filigreed gold, enamel and rock crystal.

It was later found by chance, but both its shape and purpose remain a mystery.

Inscribed in Celtic are the words:

'Alfred had me made.'

The King obviously believed it was magical, and Rock Crystal is especially lucky to whoever wears it.

Its powers certainly worked for the Monarch.

Tired and hungry, Alfred saw a rough-looking shepherd driving his sheep and goats into the meadows.

Alfred watched through the bushes as the man approached.

He knew the Danes had promised to reward anyone capturing him and he was afraid the shepherd would be tempted by the money.

However, as the shepherd drew nearer he decided he looked honest and trustworthy.

He thought he would not betray him and, anyway, he would not know that he was the King.

He therefore went up to the shepherd and begged him for food.

The moment the man looked at Alfred he knew who he was.

He knelt down and took his hand, then promised to protect him.

He offered him food and shelter in his house for which King Alfred was very grateful.

He however pointed out to the shepherd that if his neighbours saw him they too might recognise him and claim the reward.

"Do not be afraid," the shepherd said, "I will lend you

some of my clothes, then nobody will know who you are, but think you are just a poor shepherd, like me.''

Alfred agreed to this and then the shepherd went on:

''My wife is a very good woman, but it will be best that she should not know who you are, for she is rather fond of chattering to the neighbours, and she might let out the secret.''

King Alfred, dressed like a shepherd went with the shepherd to his little cottage where the man's wife was busy baking some cakes for supper.

''Here is a poor man who is very hungry,'' the shepherd said to his wife. ''Give him one of your hot cakes. He has promised to help me to look after my sheep and goats.''

The man went back to his work while his wife gave the King one of her cakes.

Thanking her he sat down on a stool to eat it, and the wife watched him.

She was thinking that he would probably eat her out of house and home if he stayed long.

After a while she said:

''I've got to go and feed the pigs. While I'm away, I'll thank you to look after the cakes which are cooking on the hearth. They will soon be brown on one side, then they will need turning. If you do that, they will be ready for my husband's supper when he comes in.''

''Willingly, good wife,'' King Alfred said with a smile.

Alfred sitting alone by the fire was thinking ironically what a strange thing it was that the King of England should be sitting in a poor shepherd's cottage helping to cook his wife's cakes.

He was wondering what had happened to his soldiers and whether he would ever be able to gather them together again and drive the Danes out of the country.

Deep in his thoughts, he forgot all about the cakes.

When the woman came back into the cottage she was horrified to find them burned to a cinder.

Furiously angry, she went behind Alfred and boxed him soundly on the ears!

"You lazy good-for-nothing rascal!" she exclaimed. "You were glad enough to eat the food I gave you, but you were too idle, it seems to keep my husband's supper from burning!"

The King apologised profusely for what he had done.

Later, when the King had conquered the Danes he did not forget the shepherd and his wife.

He sent them a bag of money in payment for the cakes he had burned.

Because his disguise had been so successful the first time, he decided to disguise himself again because he was anxious to get into a large Danish camp nearby and see if he could find out what his enemies were planning.

He was aware that he would have to be careful because if they caught him spying they would certainly kill him.

But he was determined to get into the camp himself because there was no one else he could trust.

He disguised himself as a minstrel and because he could sing and play the harp well he wandered about playing and singing to them.

He certainly cheered up the Danes who enjoyed listening to him and, in fact, they were so pleased with his music that they took him to Guthrum, their Chief, who was in a large tent of his own away from the ordinary serving men.

Guthrum was delighted with the entertainment and begged the King to stay with them for a few days.

During his stay Alfred made good use of his eyes and ears, and discovered what the Danes were plotting.

Slipping quietly out of the camp he then called together all his soldiers, and after a long and fierce battle, this time they conquered them.

Guthrum was taken prisoner and expected to be killed, but the King said he forgave them, and begged Guthrum to become a Christian and help him to defend the country from other enemies.

Guthrum was so deeply touched by the King's mercy that he replied.

"O brave King, you have disarmed me twice!"

Guthrum became a Christian and was baptised in the name of 'Athelstan'.

Alfred was the first King to have a Navy and he was very proud of it.

He sent abroad for Engineers and carpenters to show his subjects how to build ships, and paid them well.

It was King Alfred who thought of a clever way of measuring time which he did with the help of coloured candles.

They were painted in rings of different colours, red, blue, green, and yellow and he knew when one colour was melted how long he had spent on one thing.

It was a clever idea, except for the fact that when the wind blew on the flames the candle wax burnt down quicker than when it was a calm day.

It was then that King Alfred had a number of lanterns built and the candles were put inside them.

He was, therefore, the first inventor of clocks in England.

KING ALFRED THE GREAT

KING EDWARD THE CONFESSOR

KING EDWARD THE CONFESSOR
1004-1066

Save for the brief reign of King Harold of less than a year, Edward the Confessor was the King who preceded the Norman Conquest.

He founded Westminster Abbey on the site where a smaller and dilapidated Church had previously stood.

King Edward wore a sapphire ring and one day when accosted by a beggar, because he had no money, he gave the beggar his ring.

Later, two pilgrims from the Holy Land returned with the story that an old man calling himself St. John had told them that disguised as a beggar he had been given the ring by the King.

The ring was returned to King Edward and in 1066 when he died, the ring was buried with him.

Two hundred years after his death, his coffin was opened and his body was found to be in a perfect state of preservation.

The Abbot of Westminster removed the sapphire and it now adorns the centre of the cross of the British Imperial State Crown.

A religious minded mystic, King Edward after he died was Canonised in 1161 and was given a shrine in the Abbey of his origination.

QUEEN MARIA CRISTINA OF SPAIN

H.C.M. MARIA CRISTINA,
QUEEN REGENT OF SPAIN
1806-1878

Queen Maria Cristina of Bourbon-Sicily married
Ferdinand VII King of Spain, the brother of her mother.

The King's first wife had been the sister of her father.

Maria Cristina was twenty-three years old, while the King
was forty-five and had already been widowed three times.

In 1833, King Ferdinand, who she had nursed devotedly,
died and she became Queen Regent for her daughter
Isabella II.

Maria Cristina bravely defended the throne during a long
and terrible civil war.

She was very attractive, when she smiled 'every man's
heart was at her feet' and she had a passionate nature.

She met Fernando Muñoz, a Corporal in the Guards,
during an afternoon's drive.

The Queen's nose began to bleed and, having used up
her own handkerchiefs and those of her ladies-in-waiting,
they borrowed one from their escort.

When the Queen returned it to the Corporal she saw he
was a dark, muscular, noble, if somewhat sensual-looking
man.

With flamboyant chivalry he raised the blood-stained
handkerchief to his lips.

For months the Corporal haunted the ardent young
Queen's dreams until, again in a coach, she was travelling
across the snow-covered Guadarrama mountains escorted
by two officers and Corporal Muñoz.

They skidded, there was an accident, and again the
Corporal offered his handkerchief.

Later the Queen suggested a walk with one officer and
the Corporal. Some distance from the Palace she sent the
officer back for an umbrella.

Alone with the man she loved, the Queen told him of
her feelings.

That a Queen should take a lover was nothing new, but this Queen proposed marriage and Muñoz, the son of simple people who kept a tobacco shop, fell on his knees and burst into tears.

After three months of widowhood, the Queen was married secretly and was wildly, ecstatically happy.

Muñoz moved into the Palace as Groom of the Bedchamber, and unlike any other Royal favourites was not ambitious for power or title.

The Queen had four children by him and had the greatest difficulty in keeping her pregnancies hidden.

Muñoz was created Duke de Riansares, decorated with The Order of the Golden Fleece and raised to the rank of a Grandee of the First Order.

Among the many wonderful jewels owned by the Spanish Crown there was an amazingly rich sapphire and diamond necklace which was Queen Maria Cristina's favourite.

Her necklace enhanced her beauty and Muñoz continually asked her to wear it because it pleased him so much.

She had her portrait painted for him wearing this beautiful necklace which, in 1982 was sold at Christie's for $297,000.

TZAR ALEXANDER II OF RUSSIA

Tzar Alexander II succeeded his father, the Emperor Nicholas in 1855.

In 1861 he freed twenty-three-million serfs.

On his 21st birthday precious stones were discovered in the Ural mountains and named after him.

It was found that the stone changed colour according to the different rays of light, being by daylight olive, or emerald green, and in artificial light columbine or raspberry red.

As its changing colours were those of Imperial Russia, green and red, it was popular among the patriotic ladies of the country.

They believed it brought them good luck.

It is also a stone which stands for struggle and progress besides being the emblem of loyal regard.

Tzar Alexander II fell in love at the age of forty-two with the Princess Katherine Dolgoruky.

She was twelve years old at the time and was riding her pony.

In 1865, when the Dolgorukys were in St. Petersburg, the Tzar began to court Katherine with bonbons and flowers.

By now she was a slim, dark-eyed sixteen-year-old with bright chestnut hair.

A year later Katherine became his mistress.

She surrendered to him in the Imperial Pavilion in the park of the Winter Palace. Every day he managed to snatch an hour or two with her.

He became "her slave, her adorer, his life . . . his idol . . . for ever".

He drew a picture of her naked and worshipped her. They had four children.

The unhappy Tzarina died and six weeks later he married his adored Katherine with only two witnesses present.

He showered her with jewels and settled a huge fortune

and properties on her both at home and abroad.

He gave her Alexandrite, his namesake, like the perfect specimens which were in the Russian Crown Jewels.

They had been married for only eight months when on March 13th 1882 Tzar Alexander was assassinated.

Bombs were thrown beneath his carriage by Nihilists.

TZAR ALEXANDER II OF RUSSIA

H.R.H. PRINCE NAPOLEON

THE PRINCE NAPOLEON

Prince Napoleon, the brother of Emperor Napoleon III was the most sensual man in the whole of Paris.

He made all the famous Courtesans his mistresses, one after another, gave them jewellery, houses and horses, and was the most knowledgeable man on sexual passion in the whole of France.

He was exceedingly clever, but at the same time, he adored the cocottes and perhaps the most expensive of his many affairs was the one with Cora Pearl.

Strangely enough she was an English girl who had been born Eliza Emma Crouch in 1835.

She was the daughter of a Plymouth Music Teacher who left his wife and emigrated to America.

Mrs. Crouch, finding it hard to manage alone with four young children, sent Eliza to a Convent School in Boulogne.

The girl remained there for eight years and made a number of friends.

When she left School she did not live with her mother, but was sent to stay with her grand-mother in London, where she lived a 'godly, steadfast life.'

Night after night she read travel books to her aged relative and on Sundays she was escorted to Church by a maid, who waited to escort her home again.

One Sunday, for some reason the maid was not waiting for her and she started out alone for her grand-mother's house.

She was not really pretty, but very spirited with an excellent figure and red hair.

A middle-aged man followed her – a diamond merchant – who took her to a drinking den.

Foolishly, she accepted the drink he offered her.

When she recovered consciousness she found herself beside him in bed.

After that she took a number of lovers, then went to

Paris.

She was determined to appear to be worldly and managed to obtain gowns from Worth and Laferriere and jewels from the Rue de la Paix.

Her lovers grew more important and distinguished as her reputation became known.

It was the fifth Prince of Essling who obligingly bought her clothes and jewels, as well as paying for her servants.

He paid her Chef, Salé, who sometimes spent thirty thousand *francs* on food in a fortnight.

The Prince also gave her money to lose at the Baden Casino and on their visit there in 1869, she spent, apart from gambling losses, over fifty-nine thousand *francs*.

She was not faithful to the Prince of Essling and at the same time as she was giving herself to him she was also giving her favours to Prince Achille Murat, who was eleven years his junior.

Murat was not rich, but he was incapable of refusing Cora anything she desired.

This was actually her first horse and she was so thrilled with it that she took a house at 61, Rue de Ponthieu, where the stables were her pride and joy.

She had at least a dozen horses and between the years 1863 and 1868 she bought more than sixty fine saddle and carriage horses with which to ride and drive.

And she had a caleche upholstered in sky-blue.

In three years she spent ninety-thousand *francs* with one horse-dealer alone.

She played her lovers off, one against the other.

Prince Napoleon, who was besotted by her like all the others, would be told how one man had given her a neckace worth £5,000.

He would therefore buy her perhaps a riviere of diamonds worth twice as much.

Then another lover, not to be outdone, would spend even more.

Prince Napoleon gave Cora a key to the Palais Royal where he lived.

In fact she sometimes slept in the room next to that of the lady-in-waiting, and dined in the Dining-Room that was used by Princess Clothilde.

Prince Napoleon grew more and more generous.

He established Cora in an enormous house that was more like a Palace of her own which came to be known as les *Petites Tuileries*.

She bathed in a rose marble Bath-room, with her initials inlaid in gold at the bottom of the bath.

Not satisfied with one house, Cora persuaded Prince Napoleon to buy her a second maison in Paris, at 6, Rue des Bassins.

In the last five years of the Second Empire in 1865-1870, Cora was so rich that her jewels alone were worth a million *francs*.

One evening Prince Napoleon offered her a 'large vanload' of the most expensive orchids.

She gave a supper-party, strewed the orchids over the floor and, dressed like a sailor, danced the Hornpipe all over them, followed by the Can-Can.

One of her lovers presented her with a box of *marrons glacés,* each *marron* separately wrapped in a thousand-*franc* note.

Another admirer sent her an enormous silver horse which was carried in by two porters, and proved to be full of jewels and gold.

The Courtesans and the festivities of the Second Empire brought the Jewellers untold prosperity.

On his marriage in 1853 the Emperor Napoleon III had one of the crowns of diamonds reset in a modern style.

Laferriere designed an Imperial crown with eagles on it.

Unfortunately, it was not finished because, for political reasons the Coronation itself was abandoned.

All that was left was the diamond studded cross made and mounted.

While the crown itself was not finished, the jewels of the previous reign joined the cascade of precious stones displayed at the Tuileries and at Compiègne.

Tiaras became the fashion and Oscar Massin created diamond foliage and bouquets which could be compared with the finest work of any century.

Massin's jewelled flowers were sprigs of eglantine and lilies-of-the-valley which seemed to shine with a dazzling light.

The Empress bought a jewelled lilac blossom which was shown at the Exhibition in 1867.

In 1904 the jewellery of Princess Mathilde, who was the cousin of Louis-Napoleon, was sold and a seven-string pearl necklace, composed of 384 pearls, which had been Napoleon's wedding-present to her mother fetched nearly half-a-million *francs*.

The Emperor's mistress, La Castiglione, came dressed as the Queen of Sheba for a Fancy-Dress Ball.

She had 'at least a thousand precious stones flashing and shining.'

Perhaps even more dazzling than Cora Pearl was La Païva, who displayed two-million *francs* worth of diamonds, pearls and precious stones on her exquisite body.

She was a Russian and married first to a Frenchman, then to a German.

She took as her lover Herr Henckel von Donnersmarck who was closely associated with Count Otto von Bismarck.

There was no doubt that La Païva's fantastic house in the Champs Élysées was the centre of Prussian espionage.

At the time, it left all Paris breathless with its splendour.

The Salon walls were hung with crimson damask, specially woven at Lyons for eight hundred thousand *francs*.

The staircase, lit by a massive lustre of sculpted bronze was made entirely of onyx, steps, baluster and all.

The bath-room walls were of onyx and marble and the bath was solid onyx and its three taps were set with precious stones.

The locks on the doors were worth two-thousand *francs* each.

The bed was inlaid with rare woods and ivory.

It stood like an altar in an alcove under a ceiling on which Andora, Goddess of the Dawn, was painted.

It had cost a hundred-thousand *francs.*

La Païva was a symbol of the Courtesans who cared only for money, fell in love with money, and cared about nothing else.

She had a horror of dogs and cats, birds and children and anything that caused her expense but brought no rewards.

She had foreseen the coming war between France and Prussia and it was not unwelcome.

In March, 1871, when the Prussians entered Paris, every house in the Champs Élysées was locked and shuttered, except for one.

From the steps of her house, La Païva and Henckel von Donnersmarck in full uniform, watched the soldiers march past.

The fall of the Empire brought a last and final triumph for La Païva.

On the 28th October, when her marriage to her husband had been annulled, she and Henckel von Donnersmarck were married at the Lutheran Church in Paris.

She was fifty-two and her husband gave her the Empress Eugénie's necklace which, as an ex-Empress, she had been forced to sell.

The three rows of diamonds were faultless, and it was considered to be the finest example of a Jeweller's art at the time.

This is a sad end to the glitter, the extravagance and the glamour of the Second Empire.

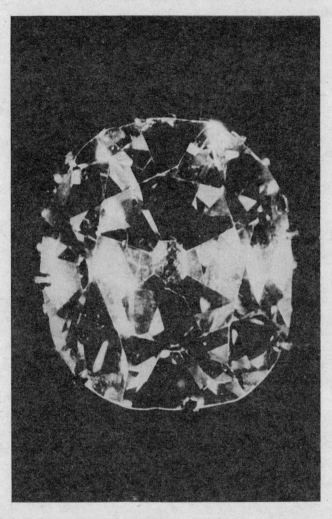

HIS EXALTED HIGHNESS THE NIZAM OF HYDERABAD

HIS EXALTED HIGHNESS THE SEVENTH NIZAM OF HYDERABAD
1894-1967

The Nizam of Hyderabad was reputed to be the richest man in the world.

The rats had secretly gnawed away in the bowels of his Palace three-million pounds worth of banknotes.

This, however, hardly affected his fortune.

In 1967 it was revealed that twenty-four million pounds of gold bars, gold coin, and over thirty-million more in jewellery was owned by the Nizam.

Two of the diamonds alone were each the size of a lemon weighed over a hundred carats.

Compared with the 'Hope' Diamond which weighed fourteen-and-a-half carats, the 'Regent' was sensational at a hundred and forty and a half and was owned by Napoleon for four-million dollars. It was, therefore, not surprising that most connoisseurs considered the 'Regent' unsaleable.

The Nizam's father actually used it as a paper-weight.

On the Nizam's death his personal fortune was estimated at between £160 million and £600 million.

His Exalted Highness, victorious in battle, shadow of God and faithful ally of the British was not a large man.

Five feet, three inches tall and very slender, he retained his youthful looks long past middle-age.

In private he wore crumpled cotton pyjamas like the common people, camel-skin slippers bought for a few shillings in the Bazaar, grey socks and a disgraceful old fez which he continued to wear on his head for thirty-five years.

He was good looking and spoke quietly, but there was something about him incalculable, something dangerous.

People said they saw it in his eyes which were black behind his cheap steel-rimmed spectacles.

He stared without blinking and without a hint of expression.

The seventh Nizam was by lineage and appointment undeniably a King.

He was related to Asaf Jah, the first of the great Nizams.

When the Nizam came to the throne he was the product of a childhood spent in the Harem in the company of women, and of a youth guided by a British Tutor.

He practised the manly exercises of a clean young Englishman, riding at a gutted sheep from an upright pole and bisecting it with a single cut.

He was thin and vigorous and preened himself in long, smooth coats buttoned with pearls, emeralds, rubies and diamonds.

As time went by the Nizam displayed a number of contradictions.

He owned one of the world's finest collections of Grecian silver, rare jade and crystal of peerless quality.

He amassed things in a fever of possession.

No luxury car was safe in Hyderabad for the Nizam would ask its owner if he might take a ride in it.

Then he would have it taken straight to his Palace and stored.

In the end the Nizam had collected more than two hundred great limousines, none with any great amount of mileage recorded.

At formal dinners in the Falaknuma Palace, even the crumb scoops were of solid gold and there was enough gold plate to feed three-hundred.

The food, because it was paid for out of public funds was lavish.

But an invitation to tea in private would mean only a frugal biscuit.

The Nizam was a heavy smoker of local cigarettes bought in the Bazaar for a few pence for a pack of ten, but his guests were offered more expensive brands left behind by previous visitors.

It was his habit to dump ashes and stubs in a neat pile near him on the floor by his side.

Yet he was meticulously clean. In his last years, he washed his hands after every letter or State paper he handled.

He was also more able to come to an assessment with regard to his possessions than any appraiser, jeweller, or civil servant.

The Nizam collected women, and it was believed that he exercised the *droit du seigneur,* a custom both ancient and well-known, especially in France.

In the part of the Harem where his mother moved there were women who were neither slaves nor servants.

They were dependents, and were called *khannazads.*

On festive occasions, like her son's birthday or a public holiday, the Dowager might select from among them a beautiful virgin, have her bathed, perfumed and dressed in gauzes and gold, and send her to him as a surprise present.

Because he could not refuse his mother's gift the girl would become part of his own household and live as a concubine in the Harem.

A family with a pretty daughter considered it a means of advancement for her to belong to the Nizam.

Whispers would pass from courtier to courtier until the good news reached the ears of His Exalted Highness.

An inspection of the entourage by some trusted woman would be arranged.

Occasionally a family might be honoured without any formality.

Such was the case with Leila Begum, a singing girl whose beauty struck the Nizam dumb while he was touring the provinces.

She became his favourite and bore him five sons and two daughters.

The Nizam had four wives as allowed by Islam.

His first, a local aristocrat, he married at the age of twenty in 1906. She had two sons who survived him, and a daughter who was not allowed to marry.

This was due to a superstition that if she left the household she would bring on her father's death.

The Nizam's first wife became a poet and made a pilgrimage to Mecca.

His third wife was a niece of the Aga Khan and the two others were drawn from the nobility of Hyderabad.

At the height of his reign the Nizam was probably the owner of some two hundred concubines and in the 1920's he took most of them with him in a special train when he visited New Delhi for a few days.

At the end of his reign the total was reduced for economic reasons, to forty-two.

The children, who numbered between fifty and one hundred and ten, remained a charge, as well as some score of *khannazads* and a thousand servants.

There was a painful problem with one daughter whose kleptomania made it necessary for her to be followed round the bazaars so that what she stole could be paid for or replaced.

The Nizam in his old age became interested in health and his chief relaxation was in watching surgical operations.

But for many years his passion was for *unani,* the medical system of ancient Greece.

The Nizam's fourth Palace, Falaknuma, he thought of as a large Guest-House for the eminent.

A visit by Royalty cost him thousands in refurbishing.

When the glamorous young Prince of Wales came to stay for three or four days in 1922, the Polo Ground was completely re-turfed and a Squash Court was built especially for His Royal Highness, but he did not use it.

At one time the large bed in the principal Suite was lengthened for the Viceroy who was very tall.

Falaknuma's style was Edwardian, with velvet plush and wine-dark glass crammed into a Grecian case of marble walls and staircases.

The Nizam placed hidden cameras in his guests' bath-rooms.

One of his legacies was a unique assortment of candid photographs of his famous guests performing their toilets.

It eventually joined his notable collection of more commonplace erotica in a back room of the Hyderabad Museum.

At the end of 1956 the Nizam retired and disappeared into obscurity, his daughter woke him at five o'clock with the first of his forty or fifty cups of coffee a day.

By seven he had composed the menus for all his household, issuing them from his cramped white-painted bed-room like Imperial writs.

The seventh Nizam's retirement lasted for more than a decade.

They were years that were lightened by the presence in his ménage of a small white goat.

It had been injured by his car and nursed back to health by the best medical facilities of the Palace.

Now it sat by the Nizam's side on the verandah, munching turnips while he nibbled betel nuts and drank the dark juice of poppies.

Soon after the goat died the Nizam also expired. He was eighty-one.

In the hot white streets half a million of the people in Hyderabad mourned the passing not of a man, but of a symbol.

THE GRAND DUCHESS VLADIMIR OF RUSSIA

THE GRAND DUCHESS VLADIMIR OF RUSSIA

The Grand Duchess Vladimir became the leading hostess in St. Petersburg where she held Court in her magnificent Vladimir Palace on the Neva river.

Her collection of jewels were spectacular although not as fabulous as those of the Dowager Empress Marie Feodorovna.

In the Russian style they were displayed to her guests.

When Consuelo Vanderbilt, who became the Duchess of Marlborough visited St. Petersburg in 1902, she wrote in her diary:

"After dinner the Grand Duchess showed me her jewels set out in glass cases in her dressing-room. There were endless parures of diamonds, emeralds, rubies and pearls, to say nothing of semi-precious stones such as turquoises, tourmalines, cat's eyes and aquamarines."

At the time of the Revolution in 1908 the Grand Duchess went to Kislovodsk in the Caucusus, which was still in the hands of loyal Cossack troops.

Towards the end of 1919 she made her escape by horse-drawn carriage and train, finally settling in Zurich.

She had taken a case of jewels with her when she left St. Petersburg, but the bulk of her collection had been left walled up in the Vladimir Palace.

A young Englishman called Stopford, disguised as an old woman, enlisted the help of one of her loyal retainers to get him into the Palace at night.

The secret safe had not been found by the looters and he removed the jewels.

He wrapped the priceless pieces in newspapers and stuffed them into old Gladstone bags.

He hid in his black bonnet a tiara, cramming fifteen pearl drops of it into the cherries that were sewn on as trimming.

Having been attached to the British Embassy, Stopford, by using diplomatic channels managed to get all the jewels out of Russia.

QUEEN MARY

QUEEN MARY, CONSORT OF KING GEORGE V
1867-1953

Queen Mary was 5 feet 6 inches tall, although she looked taller because of her perfect posture.

She had flawless shoulders and a skin like alabaster.

She always wore pale colours and her favourite colour was pale blue.

When she was young, her hair was honey-coloured, but because it was so fine she always wore a hairpiece when she wished to attach a tiara, which she did every night for dinner, even if she was only dining alone with the King.

It was said of Queen Mary:

". . . I have never known an Empress or a Queen who could wear a quantity of superb jewels with such ease and simplicity and without appearing in the least overladen . . ."

It is due to Queen Mary's careful planning that the Royal Family's collection of jewellery exists in its present form today.

She received a large amount of jewellery as Wedding gifts in 1893. In 1897 her mother died and she inherited some of her diamonds.

She and King George were given precious jewels during their long tours of the Empire.

Then Queen Alexander, following the death of her husband, passed on to Queen Mary the jewels which Queen Victoria had left to the Crown.

In 1910 Queen Mary was also given the 102 cleavings of the Cullinan diamond as a gift by the South African Government.

She received her mother's Cambridge emeralds on the death of her brother Prince Francis.

In 1911 there were magnificent gifts to celebrate King George's Coronation in June, and in December at the Delhi Durbar the King and Queen were given fabulous treasures from the vaults of the Maharajahs.

Then in 1929 Queen Mary bought some of the fabulous jewels worn by the Royal Family today.

When George, Duke of York married Princess May of Teck, as she then was, he was very fond of her, but not in love.

However, their love grew and deepened with the years as the following letters show:

George, Duke of York to Princess May of Teck:

York Cottage,
Sandringham.

1894.

" . . . You know by this time that I never do anything by halves. When I asked you to marry me I was very fond of you, but not very much in love with you, but I saw in you the person I was capable of loving most deeply, if only you could return that love . . .

I have tried to understand you and to know you, and with the happy result that I know now that I do love you, darling girl, with all my heart, and am simply devoted to you . . .

I adore you sweet May.

George."

Princess Mary (she was called Mary only after she married) replied to one of George's letters:

" . . . What a pity it is that you cannot tell me what you write, for I should appreciate it so enormously . . ."

On becoming King in May 1910 George wrote in his diary:

"God will help me in my great responsibilities and darling May will be my comfort as she has always been."

TZAR PETER III OF RUSSIA

Peter was born under an unlucky star.

One of the Empress Elizabeth's first acts upon her accession to the throne was to send to Holstein for the Duchess of Holstein-Gottorp's only child, Peter.

Although the Empress immediately announced the thirteen-year-old boy to be her heir, his appearance gave her somewhat of a shock.

The Grand Duke Peter was a pathetic creature.

He was plain and thin with lank blond hair, combed straight down over his collar.

He held himself erect and talked in a high voice of piercing intensity.

He made ugly grimaces and had a lolling tongue.

It took the Empress some time to discover that the truth was that the boy's nervousness was due to the fact that his brain had been permanently damaged by the cruelty of the Holstein 'Governors' who were employed to look after him following his father's death.

Ever since his earliest years, he had been beaten and tormented.

He was sometimes made to kneel down on sacks of peas until his legs were red and bruised.

The Empress found Tutors and told them to educate him, but they soon came to the conclusion that they were dealing with a mind that was retarded and damaged, so that it was impossible to hold his attention.

Peter played the violin a little, but what he liked best was drilling his hundreds of toy soldiers.

He made all his attendants enter into games with him and spent his days in a miniature world of battles and glory.

When Peter became sixteen the Empress decided to find him a wife.

She sought the advice of Frederick the Great and sent for the daughter of a Prussian soldier — Prince Anhalt-Zerbst.

With astonishing alacrity Sophia Augusta Frederika

arrived in St. Petersburg accompanied by her mother.

Sophia changed her name to Catherine upon adopting the Orthodox faith, and became known in history as Catherine the Great.

In her memoirs she wrote:

"I was in my fifteenth year and the Grand Duke showed himself very assiduous for the first ten days.

In that short space of time I became aware that he was not very enamoured of the great nation over which he was destined to rule. He was a convinced Lutheran, did not like his entourage and was very childish. I kept silent and listened, which helped to gain his confidence. I remember that he told me amongst other things that what he liked most in me was that I was his second cousin and in that capacity, as a relative, he could talk freely to me; after this he confided that he was in love with one of the Empress's ladies-in-waiting.

He would have liked to marry her, but had resigned himself to marrying me, as his Aunt wished it."

Cathrine admits:

"I did not care about Peter, but I did about the Crown."

She put herself out to please the Empress and a year later she was married to the Grand Duke in a ceremony of dazzling grandeur.

The Empress was determined to impress upon the onlookers the glory of her Court.

She gave all the public officials a year's salary in advance and compelled them to spend a large part of it on equipment for the pageant.

Those who came first in the hierarchy were ordered to have not less than eight lackeys attached to each carriage and as many more as could be afforded.

Catherine wrote that the marriage was never consummated, and explained:

" . . . the ladies undressed me and put me to bed . . . Everybody left me and I remained alone for more than two hours, not knowing what was expected of me.

Should I get up? Should I remain in bed? I truly did not know. At last Madame Krause, my new maid, came in and told me very cheerfully that the Grand Duke was waiting for his supper which would be served shortly. His Imperial Highness came to bed after supper and began to say how amused the servants would be to find us in bed together. Madame Krause questioned us the next day about our marital experiences, but she was disappointed in her hopes."

Catherine was to learn that the Grand Duke spent all his time playing soldiers in his room with his Valets performing a great deal of exercises and changing their uniforms three times a day.

As time passed Catherine was careful to hide the excrutiating boredom she found at the Court where she said that half the people could not read and only a third could write.

The Grand Duke Peter however, managed to alleviate the tedium by boring holes in the floor of his apartment and peering into his Aunt, the Empress's private apartments, where he could watch her making love.

When Peter came to the throne as Tzar his mistress, Elizabeth Petrovna, gave him a large and beautiful emerald, which gained the reputation of being an unlucky gem.

Soon after receiving it Peter was murdered, and it was rumoured that he was in fact, killed by his wife's lover Gregory Orloff.

The next person to wear it was Emperor Paul, who was strangled.

Alexander II was assassinated and the stone fell from his finger.

Alexander III would not wear it, but Nicholas charmed by its beauty, did.

He had a reign full of trouble and finally a Revolution in 1917 overthrew the Romanovs and they were shot, in 1918.

No one knows what became of this fatal emerald.

TZAR PETER III OF RUSSIA

H.M. QUEEN MARIE OF YUGOSLAVIA
1900-1961

The Royal Jewels of Yugoslavia were very beautiful and Queen Marie looked lovely in the Tiara which was made of diamonds with enormous capusson emeralds encircling it, which originally came from Russia.

Yet perhaps the emeralds were unlucky to Queen Marie.

The daughter of King Ferdinand I of Roumania and Princess Maria of Great Britain and Ireland, and of Saxe-Coburg and Gotha, she lived in the exciting country which has inspired so many novels.

Princess Marie had two sisters and three brothers, and her eldest brother was Prince Carol.

He was tall, handsome and intelligent, he was not lacking in a sense of duty as at the age of nineteen he helped his mother in a cholera camp

However in 1918 he made a run away marriage with a Colonel's daughter, known as Zizi. The marriage was annulled and he assumed his position as Heir Apparent and fell in love with the beautiful Princess Helen of Greece.

They were married and his whole family rejoiced.

To their utter despair he eloped again with the redheaded Elena Lupescu and Crown Prince Carol renounced the throne of Yugoslavia in order to be with his Mistress.

Princess Marie who was very pretty and shy, and very unlike her brother married in 1922 H.M. King Alexander I, King of Yugoslavia.

She was very happy with him and they had three sons, Prince Peter born in 1923, Prince Tomislav born 1928, and Prince Andrej born in 1929.

Yugoslavia is the largest country in the Balkan Peninsula, It was created by Peace Treaties in 1919 out of States administered by Austria and Hungary.

Both were notorious as Europe's oldest trouble spots. Also among the new Nation's constituents was the Kingdom of Serbia.

For centuries Serbia had been restless by the rival claims

of two dynasties both of peasant origin.

One was the Karadjordjevics (Kara Djordje or "Black George" which was the nickname of his Founder) and the other was the Obrenovics.

In 1903 the King of the Obrenovics, Alexander, became unpopular with the army and the powerful Radical Party because he had married his mistress, a fascinating woman called Draga Masin.

Troops broke into the Palace in Belgrade and murdered Alexander and Draga and threw their bodies into the garden, where they lay exposed while Officers sat at their table in the Palace drinking to their new King Peter Karadjordjevic.

It was Peter Kardjordjevic who in 1919 was promoted to the throne of the new Serbo-Croat-Slovene Kingdom. The name of Yugoslavia did not come into use until 1929.

King Peter aged 74 and in uncertain health, was only titular King, with his son Alexander acting as Prince Regent.

The old man believed in constitutional rule but his son although with good intentions, had dictatorial tendencies.

Serious looking, older than his years wearing pince-nez glasses Alexander succeeded his father in 1921.

He ran into trouble with the Croats seeking independence, but he decided in 1929 to save the country he must take over himself.

He suspended the Constitution, changed the name of the country to Yugoslavia and dismissed Parliament, declaring that the time had come when no one should stand between the people and their King.

He divided Yugoslavia into nine countries. His Police were brutal, the Peasant and the Communist Parties were victimised and Croatian frustration turned to violence.

In 1934 when he arrived in Marseille for a State visit to France King Alexander was shot dead by a Bulgarian assassin hired by a Croatin terrorist group. The French Foreign Minister was also killed in the attack.

This meant that King Alexander's eldest son Peter who

was only eleven years old, came to the Throne.

His cousin Prince Paul a clever and accomplished man who was more interested in art than in Government agreed to act as Regent until Peter reached his eighteenth birthday.

With the second World War looming in the Balkans King Peter had only two years more to reach his majority.

Prince Paul was in a frightening position, as he was strongly pro-British, having been at Oxford, lived in London as a young man, and also he had married the sister of the Duchess of Kent.

But six of the seven States bordering Yugoslavia had thrown in their lot with Nazi Germany.

The country could not defend itself and the Croats were ready to defect.

There were only two alternatives, either German or Russian domination.

With a heavy heart Prince Paul signed a pact with Germany and Italy in March 1941. Two days later there was a Military Revolt encouraged by the British Government, in which the Yugoslav Government was overthrown.

King Peter II was invested with powers which six months later he would have assumed on his eighteenth birthday.

Hitler ordered an immediate attack on Yugoslavia and Greece, but Belgrade had nine days of Peace and King Peter was crowned amid hysterical scenes of rejoicing.

But on April 6th the Luftwaffe struck and on April 17th King Peter followed Prince Paul into exile.

King Peter headed a Yugoslavian Government in Exile in London and won his wings in the British Royal Air Force.

He wished to be parachuted into Yugoslavia to join the Resistance Movement led by Tito, but he was refused.

At the close of the War King Peter was not allowed to return to his country and by the end of 1945 the Communist Party was dominant and Yugoslavia a Federal People's Republic.

King Peter went into Exile in America until his death at Colorado in 1970.

Queen Marie as she was English had come to England with her three young sons and had settled in a small village in Bedforshire where she was very lonely when they were at school, and had only Ladies-in-Waiting and two Yugoslav servants to look after her.

She was only too anxious to do anything she could to help the War effort and she visited a great number of camps and secret Stations, where the women, W.A.A.F.S. and A.T.S. particularly, were thrilled to meet a Queen.

When her son King Peter went into Exile in America he took with him the Royal Jewels of Yugoslavia.

Queen Marie was very sad that he was forced to sell them so that he could support his wife Princess Alexandra of Greece and Denmark, and their son Crown Prince Alexander who was born in 1945.

QUEEN MARIE OF YUGOSLAVIA

TZAR IVAN THE TERRIBLE

TZAR IVAN THE TERRIBLE
1530-1584

Ivan was crowned as the first Tzar of Russia in 1547. He was the very wealthy Sovereign of a very poor country.

When an English traveller called Fletcher was shown the Tzar's treasure, he thought he must be dreaming.

Great heaps of pearls, emeralds, and rubies lay amongst piles of gold plate and hundreds of gold cups were enriched with gems and precious stones of every kind.

These riches, which had been constantly amassed from reign to reign, were generally kept hidden away.

They were shown only on special occasions, usually to impress foreigners.

On the departure of an Embassy to Poland, five-hundred horsemen were dressed with a magnificence that exceeded all imagination.

Their garments were of gold and silver tissue, their saddle housings of pearl embroidered velvet.

But the Tzar's Palace was little more than a hut, despite the fact that it was described to outsiders as the 'Palace of Gold'.

The Sovereign sat on a throne borne by four creatures modelled on the fantastic monsters of the Apocalypse.

He ate at a massive gold table and was brought a hundred dishes of gold and silver all at the same time.

As he lay dying in 1584 Ivan picked up some turquoises and said:

"See how they change colour! They are turning paler. They foretell my death."

QUEEN ALEXANDRA

QUEEN ALEXANDRA
1844-1925

The Princess of Wales, Princess Alexandra, was fifty-seven when she became Queen Consort on the accession of H.M. King Edward VII.

Queen Alexandra epitomised the popular concept of a Queen clothed in a shimmering haze of precious gems.

In the daytime she wore just a *sautoir* and a small brooch on her collar.

During the evening, however, she glittered with jewels.

She wore a tiara, a high pearl dog-collar and rows of sparkling diamond chains.

Pinned to her gowns were brooches — stars, crescents, butterflies and flowers.

She also wore earrings and a number of bracelets over her white kid gloves.

On State occasions Queen Alexandra appeared to be covered in jewels from the top of her head to the hem of her gown.

When she entered Westminster Abbey for the Coronation it was said she sparkled as if she was 'ablaze with light'.

Queen Alexandra was not oblivious to the effect she created.

When a function was arranged for the last day of official mourning for Queen Victoria, her ladies asked if they could change from their black for this special occasion.

She refused to give a ruling on the matter knowing that her ladies would not appear in anything but black without her permission.

Queen Alexandra however, wore white and sparkled with jewels,

She was an outstandingly beautiful woman and it was Margot Asquith who said that 'she always made other women look common'.

She was also said to possess the world's 'most perfect

shoulders and bosom for the display of jewels'.

In fact, the portrait painter Philip de Laszlo wrote after painting the King and Queen at Windsor:

"I particularly admired the grace of her movements. Personally I should like to have had the opportunity of painting her in evening dress, for she had very well constructed shoulders and bust, but I had to do the portrait in ordinary day dress, with a high lace collar and pearls."

Queen Victoria, 'The Matchmaker of Europe', was looking for a suitable bride for her son Albert Edward, The Prince of Wales.

When the daughter of Prince Christian of Denmark was suggested the Queen was against a Danish marriage and wrote:

". . . not a word can, I believe, be breathed against the mother, but against her father and sisters, plenty!!"

However, when she and the Prince Consort were shown a picture of Princess Alexandra, the Prince Consort exclaimed:

"From the photograph I would marry her at once!"

The Queen remarked:

"The one of Princess Alexandra is indeed lovely. What a pity she is who she is!"

Eventually Queen Victoria agreed that the Prince of Wales should marry the Princess as she knew that Prince Albert approved of the idea.

They finally met at Speyer.

As the family were admiring the beauties of the Speyer Cathedral in the Chapel of St. Bernard, they came upon the Prince of Wales accompanied by his sister and her husband.

After the meeting the Prince of Wales wrote:

"We met the Prince and Princess Christian and the young lady of whom I had heard so much and I can now candidly say that I think her charming and very pretty."

There were people who were anxious that the marriage should not take place. Scandal about Princess Alexandra and her family circulated freely.

The story of the scrofulous scar on her neck was revived.

Princess Louise of Prussia insisted that both Prince and Princess Christian were undesirable characters.

She added:

"The father is a drunkard and for some time the mother bore a very bad reputation."

These tales were exposed as fabrications.

The Prince of Wales at last decided that he would marry Alexandra and when walking in the garden of King Leopold at Laeken he proposed.

Princess Alexandra accepted him at once, but he asked her not to be too hasty and to consider.

"I did that long ago," she replied.

He asked her if she was sure she liked him well enough to become his wife and she replied:

"Yes."

Then she kissed him.

The Prince of Wales was delighted by the praise of Alexandra which was enthusiastic and met him on every side.

After their marriage the Queen was filled with joy and she wrote to King Leopold:

"... the effect of his sweet wife has already been most favourable on Bertie ..."

In 1870 the Prince of Wales became ill with typoid fever.

He lay unconscious, and near to death, but the Princess never left his bedside.

When at last he was showing signs of getting better, the Princess wrote to Princess Louise:

"... you knew what I suffered in my utter despair and misery — you would hardly know me now in my happiness. We are **never** apart and are enjoying our second honeymoon. **Never, never,** can I thank God enough for all His mercy when He listened to my prayers and gave me back my life's happiness."

When King Edward VII died in 1910, his wife, who had been forced to share him in so many ways, felt that now for a day or two he was hers and hers alone.

The Funeral was not held until a fortnight after the King's death, partly because of Alexandra's extreme reluctance to part from her husband's body.

Queen Alexandra had a heart attack on the 19th November 1925.

Her son King George V and Queen Mary were already at Sandringham, but her Grandsons reached there too late.

'Mother dear', as she liked her children to call her, was dead.

EMPEROR BOKASSA OF THE CENTRAL AFRICAN EMPIRE
b. 1921

Emperor Bokassa's lavish Coronation in December 1977 was intended to establish him as an imposing presence in Africa.

His crown alone cost over three-million pounds and the total cost of the celebrations was nearly eighteen-million pounds.

Bokassa used the equivalent of twelve month's development aid from France for this extravagant display.

Meanwhile his subjects were slaving in diamond mines and coffee plantations to earn a paltry £16.50 *a year*.

Jean Badel Bokassa had seized power in this former French Colony from his brother-in-law in 1965.

On Mother's Day in 1971 he released all women prisoners, but ordered the execution of all men convicted of assaults on women.

By 1972 he declared himself Life President as across his chest he wore forty-eight medals only two of which were legitimate, having been won with the French Army in Vietnam.

His people may have been classified by the United Nations as one of the twenty-five poorest nations in the world, but Bokassa owned five Castles and eight other properties in France, a mansion on the Riviera and a Villa in Switzerland, where he got the metal badge of a Swiss Ski resort which he wore as one of his medals.

He also had Palaces all over his own country as well as a fleet of superb limousines.

But he wanted more and in 1976, he renamed the Central African Republic an Empire, declared himself Emperor and began plans for his Coronation.

He had already erected statues of himself at every crossroads in the capital of Bangui, so it was expected that his Coronation would be lavish, although no one could have imagined quite how gross a spectacle it was to prove.

The ceremony was modelled on Napoleon's crowning in 1804 and this absurdly inappropriate idea for equatorial Africa kept French craftsmen profitably employed for months before the day itself.

An eight-ton gilded carriage was constructed in a workshop near Nice. It was made in the shape of a golden eagle.

Other coaches were made of glass and gilt.

Guiselin made his robes, the cloak and train of which was thirty-nine feet long and encrusted with 785,000 pearls.

The Paris Couturiers who made him ten Napoleonic uniforms also made 5,000 others for his Army.

His consort wore a gold lamé gown which was studded with three-quarters of a million pearls.

There were 2,000 diamonds in his crown and he carried a six-foot long bejewelled sceptre.

His throne incorporated a gilded eagle with a fifteen-foot wingspan.

Two-thousand yards of scarlet tapestry draped the Bangui Cathedral, there were twelve triumphal arches, an eight-foot high iced cake and thirty-five dappled grey horses brought specially from Normandy at a cost of £2,350 each to draw the carriage from the Palace to the crowning.

The Pope refused Bokassa's invitation to crown him, so he did the job himself.

Every beggar was ordered from the streets of the Capital as the procession wound its way down a route patrolled by women soldiers of the Imperial Guard wearing black rubber boots, black skirts and red tunics.

The Coronation took place in a sports stadium and as his attendants sweltered in temperatures in excess of 100 degrees, the procession went to the Palace for the banquet.

On their way they passed a graveyard filled with the bodies of children unfortunate enough to be born in a country where one in five infants die before their first birthday.

But that did not perturb Bokassa or his 5,000 guests.

They dined on caviare, antelope, foie gras, crayfish,

Mouton Lafite Rothschild at £70 a bottle, 150 tons of other wines and 24,000 bottles of champagne costing £200 a head.

After this outrageous extravagance Bokassa continued in his eccentricities.

Soon there were reports that he was demanding a rake off from his country's industries, feeding his opponents to the crocodiles, maintaining a Harem of young girls and ruling with corrupt brutality.

He banned the foreign press from the country, but still the stories leaked out and in September 1979, while he was visiting Libya, Bokassa was deposed amid allegations that he had personally killed some of the one hundred schoolchildren massacred in a prison six months before.

The new Government prepared an indictment against him which included mass murder, embezzlement and even cannibalism and Bokassa was sentenced to death in his absence.

By 1985 his money was virtually all gone and most of his hangers-on and relations had scattered.

The ex-Emperor found himself living with a shrunken retinue in a tumble-down Château outside Paris.

The telephone had been cut off and there was no electricity. He was left with one wife and most of his children had gone.

Three were in care after they had been caught shop-lifting for food.

Then to everybody's surprise he suddenly left France and secretly made his way back to his own country.

He may have thought he would be welcomed with open arms and swept back to power on a wave of popular enthusiasm.

Perhaps he found a life of penury in France no longer bearable.

Whatever delusions he may have had, as he stepped out of the aircraft there was a reception committee consisting of Lt.-Col. Claude Mansion and an elite corps of the Presidential Guard.

Bokassa was under arrest.

EMPEROR BOKASSA OF CENTRAL AFRICA

QUEEN MARGHERITA OF ITALY

One of the most splendid collections of pearls belonged to the Dowager Queen Margherita of Italy, whose name signifies pearl.

She had always been fond of the ocean jewel.

Her husband, King Humbert made her many presents and always gave her one special pearl every year.

In her picture she is wearing her magnificent twelve-strings of pearls, a pearl bracelet, and a pearl tiara with pear-shaped tips.

At the Coronation of H.M. King Edward VII and Queen Alexandra, as well as her Imperial Crown, the Queen wore many of her richest and most beautiful jewels.

Included were seven rows of pearls, each twenty-four to thirty inches in length, five large neck circlets of diamonds and a great corsage ornament which covered her entire bodice.

At her waist there was a splendid ornament of diamonds with large, pear-shaped pearls.

QUEEN MARGHERITA OF ITALY

KING EDWARD VII
1814-1910

Edward, Prince of Wales married Princes Alexandra of Denmark in 1863.

He had to wait a long time before he could succeed to the throne as his Mother, Queen Victoria only died in 1901.

The King's Coronation, however, after so many years of waiting, had to be postponed because he had appendicitis.

He was the first person to have a successful operation for it.

He was finally crowned on August 9th, 1901.

He was as popular a King as he had been as Prince of Wales and worked continually for the preservation of the peace of Europe.

It was because of his friendly intercourse with the heads of other nations that he earned the title 'Edward the Peacemaker'.

The King's sceptre dates back to the restoration of the Stuarts in 1660.

Its head was changed however when King Edward inserted in it the largest cut diamond ever known.

The Cullinan Diamond was discovered in the Premier Mine near Pretoria and was named after the Chairman of the Company, Sir Thomas Cullinan.

This beautiful diamond was purchased by the Transvaal Government to present to King Edward VII on his birthday.

It was eventually cut into hundreds of stones.

It is the large drop brilliant that adorns the sceptre; the square brilliant in the Royal Crown.

It was renamed 'Star of Africa' at the request of King George V.

KING EDWARD VII

TZARINA ALEXANDRA FEODOROVNA

One of the most famous of Fabergé Imperial Easter Eggs was made as a gift from Tzar Nicholas II to his wife Alexandra Feodorovna.

The Tzar and his wife were very much in love, and he heaped jewels on her to show her how deep was his love.

Amongst all the magnificent jewels, which he gave to her one day in the garden of the Winter Palace was the most wonderful Imperial Easter Egg of pale mauve matt enamel.

It was latticed with diamond ribbons, and it opened to reveal a white gold swan floating on an aquamarine lake.

Being very much younger than her husband, the Tzarina treated her jewels like toys, and she would take them out, lovingly admire them, and touch them. She was always amused by making the little Swan swim across the lake.

She little knew that when it came into the possession of King Farouk of Egypt, it would be treated roughly.

When King Farouk was sent into exile, all his treasures were auctioned. When the Curators from Sotheby's arrived to catalogue the collection, they found that the Guards protecting all the valuable items, were playing football with the famous Imperial Egg, which fortunately sustained very little damage.

Tzar Nicholas gave his wife an Imperial Easter Egg made by Fabergé every year.

On the fifteenth anniversary of the Tzar's Coronation depicted on the egg were scenes from the past fifteen years of their reign.

One of the scenes was the Coronation of Tzar Nicholas, in the Uspensky Cathedral in the Kremlin. The Crown used weighed nine pounds and it rested on the place on his forehead where a fanatical Japanese had stabbed him a few years earlier.

This caused him a tremendous headache throughout the rest of the ceremony which lasted for hours.

One of the most significant events for the Tzar and his family was the Canonization of St. Seraphim, who was an eighteenth century hermit and monk.

St. Seraphim was particularly associated with many miraculous healings whilst he was alive, and especially that of the Great-Grandmother of Nicholas II.

The Tzarina shared in the Canonization of St. Seraphim and prayed to him in deep devotion. She asked him to intercede for her saying that she badly wanted a son.

In 1904 Tzarevitch Alexis was born, and the scene of the Canonization was also depicted in miniature on the Egg.

When the Tzar arrived in Sarov for the Ceremony a letter was handed to him. It had been written by the Monk and was addressed to the *'Fourth Tzar to visit Sarov'*.

Nicholas II opened the letter.

When he read it he turned white, and never let anyone see the contents.

However those near to him knew that it contained a prophesy of a Revolution and the destruction of Orthodox Russia.

The date was the 17th July, exactly fifteen years before the execution of the Russian Royal Family on July 17th 1918.

TZARINA ALEXANDRA FEODOROVNA

KING JAMES I

JAMES I OF ENGLAND
1566-1625

James I was the King of England and Scotland.

He was the son of Mary Stuart and succeeded to the English throne on the death of Queen Elizabeth I in 1603.

Numerous plots were formed against him including the Gunpowder Plot in 1605, which is still marked today as children make huge bonfires and light fireworks on what is called 'Guy Fawkes' night on November 5th.

He persecuted the Puritans, granted many monopolies, and had the Authorised Version of The Bible published.

He was described by Henry IV of France as 'the wisest fool in Christendom'.

Nicolas de Sancy sold his diamond to James I which is how it became part of the British Crown.

Its story is fascinating.

This 55-carat diamond was bought in Constantinople in the 16th Century by Nicolas de Sancy.

The French Ambassador to Turkey, he later became Minister of Finance under Henry IV who was always short of funds.

He begged Sancy to mortgage the diamond at a Swiss Bank.

Sancy sent the stone to Switzerland in the care of a faithful servant.

On his way, at Saulieu, the servant was attacked, robbed and killed.

Sancy was desperate at having lost the servant, but he could not imagine the man letting himself be robbed of the Sancy diamond.

He therefore had the body dissected and the diamond was found in the corpse's stomach.

When Queen Henriette Maria, the daughter of Henry IV went into exile in her native France, following the defeat of Charles I by Oliver Cromwell, she took the diamond with her.

Destitute, she sold the diamond to the French.

At his death he left the gem to Louis XIV. Now part of the Crown Jewels of France, it was stolen with other jewellery in the burglary of 1792 and disappeared.

After the Revolution it turned up as part of the collection of Prince Demidov, an eccentric and cruel Russian millionaire, but it is a mystery as to how he acquired it.

Many years later the Sancy was bought by a Maharajah and taken to India, where he was trampled to death by one of his own elephants.

The Sancy was then sold to the first Lord Astor, but in 1978 his grandson negotiated its sale with the then President of France, Valery Giscard d'Estaing.

It is now in the Louvre.

MARIE ANTOINETTE—QUEEN OF FRANCE
1755-1793

When Marie Antionette first came to France she innocently asked the function of "that pretty woman who sat next to the King." She was soon enlightened.

From that moment the Dauphin dismissed Madame Du Barry and the Court was divided into two factions.

Louis and Marie Antoinette were married in the gilt and white chapel of Versailles.

The Bridegroom wore a suit of cloth of gold, spangled with diamonds, the bride wore white brocade a 'symphony of rose, gold and silver and all sparkling with diamonds'.

One of the guests present noticed that 'the corps of her robe was too small and left quite a broad strip of lacing and shift quite visible, which had a bad effect between two broader strips of diamonds'.

Rain unfortunately postponed the firework display.

The bride's only real sadness came from the apparent coldness of her husband. His grandfather The King was heard to remark,

"He's not like other men!"

The Royal couple were escorted to bed. The Archbishop of Rheims blessed the bed, the King handed the Dauphin his nightshirt and the Duchess de Chartres helped Marie Antoinette put on her nightgown.

The Hangings were drawn and then suddenly, following tradition, opened again. This was the last of the days when the consummation itself was witnessed.

As it happened there was an argument over the exact date when Louis and Marie Antoinette actually became husband and wife.

It was usually agreed it was during an August night some seven years after their marriage in 1777.

This was because Louis required surgery and fearing being operated on, he continually delayed it until Marie Antoinette's brother, the Emperor Joseph persuaded him to do so for the sake of the alliance.

The operation was successful and Marie Antoinette bore their first child the following year.

It was perhaps her lack of normal sex with her husband that made Marie Antoinette a natural flirt, seek the giddy but disastrous round of pleasure.

As a member of the Anti-Austria faction in Versailles Madame du Barry did her best to wreck the marriage.

Most of the people in Paris hated Madame du Barry, and Marie Antoinette's popularity rose because they learnt of her stand against the King's Mistress.

The Nobility had lost respect for the King and therefore they pinned all their hopes on the Dauphin and his young wife.

Marie Antoinette's smile charmed and attracted, her bearing and the proud carriage of her head made the people all admire her.

They certainly felt that her complexion which 'was literally a blend of lilies and roses' was very different from that of the other women at Court.

When she became Queen Marie Antoinette wrote to her Mother:

"I shall try to commit as few faults as I possibly can. Little by little I want and hope to correct myself. Without ever meddling in intrigue, I wish to be worthy of my husband's confidence."

The three years following the accession were the years of folly — often serious, sometimes frivolous, they destroyed her public reputation.

At one time it was said that she lighted her bedroom each night with 1,000 candles, and that she had a room with the walls dripping with diamonds.

She dressed in a flamboyant manner, and she owed the Court Jeweller half a million francs.

Her virtues were forgotten while her mistakes however small, were seized on by her enemies and magnified.

They never forgot she was an Austrian and her nationality was presented almost as a crime.

Libellous pens used the current term for lesbianism which

was *'le vice Allemand'* – the German vice, as a weapon against Marie Antoinette.

She was finally ruined through slander.

From the moment she set foot in France she was a victim of a vicious and sustained assassination of character which gradually and inevitably took her to the Guillotine.

A necklace made of diamonds, which was known as the 'Queen's Necklace' sparked off the loudest and most violent scandal of the 18th Century.

In 1785 the *Comtesse* de la Motte, who was an adventuress, had the necklace, which was the most expensive jewel of the whole era, delivered to her.

In return, she was supposed to take it to Queen Marie Antoinette, but instead she actually stole it.

Her unwilling accomplice was Prince Louis de Rohan, Cardinal and Head Chaplain of France.

He was arrested at the Palace of Versailles as he left, having just performed Mass.

Another accomplice, Cagliostro, who was both shady and untrustworthy, was also imprisoned.

The *Comtesse* de la Motte was publicly whipped and had branded on her shoulder the fleur-de-lys, which was the symbol of Royal justice.

Unfortunately and very unfairly, her trial compromised Queen Marie Antoinette although she knew nothing of what had happened and was completely innocent.

With great cleverness the *Comtesse* escaped from prison and took refuge in England.

When she reached London, she sold the diamonds a large number of which she had removed from the necklace.

She died in 1791, but there is a story that she lived for a long time under an assumed name in Odessa where she enjoyed the secret protection of the Tzar of Russia.

Twenty-one of the large diamonds she sold in London are now the property of Clare, Duchess of Sutherland.

QUEEN MARIE ANTOINETTE

MARIA PIA OF SAVOY
CONSORT OF DOM LUIZ I KING OF PORTUGAL

The beautiful Queen Maria Pia of Savoy was married to Dom Luiz I, King of Portugal.

She was the daughter of the great Victor Emmanual II (1820-1878) King of Sardinia and of Italy.

She was an immensely popular Queen who played her part with tremendous dignity.

One day, she had a *Te Deum* in Lisbon postponed by half-an-hour in order that the sunlight should fall through the stained glass windows at the exact angle to catch her red hair the moment she entered the Sanctuary.

In 1876 she commissioned this beautiful diadem of stars set with large diamonds.

She was whimsical, a spendthrift and stylish. It is easy to imagine her delight when wearing this glorious crown on top of her red hair.

King Luiz developed into a blond, podgy little man who looked like a Comic Opera Admiral in the uniform he always wore.

He was overtaken by sciatica and dropsy complaints which he aggravated by eating huge plates of meat in the mistaken belief that he needed them to keep up his strength.

But as Queen Victoria said — "People could not help liking him."

He was popular even when a revolution took place for it was evident to all that, if he did little good, at least he meant no harm.

But he could not govern Portugal, and did not appear to try to do so.

Maria Pia on the other hand, was cast in a different mould, being the daughter of a King who took himself seriously as a great man.

When Marshal Saldanha tried to start a Revolution a few shots were fired in the Palace Square, then he took over the Seals of Office before demanding an audience with the Queen.

She sent for him and spoke her mind, saying:

"Marshal, I have sent for you to say that, if I were King, I should have you shot tomorrow in a public square. Now you may go. I have told you what I think of your behaviour."

At this time Maria Pia was a girl of twenty-three — Saldanha was an eighty-year-old warrior with a venerable bald head, flashing eyes, a ferocious white moustache, and a military reputation.

But nothing daunted, Maria Pia spoke to him as a Headmaster might have spoken to an impertinent schoolboy summoned to his presence to be reprimanded.

The Marshal was in no danger and he knew it.

It would have been easier for him to have had Maria Pia shot in the public square.

But he admired her nerve.

The young woman had the *beau role* at the interview and the old fire-eater knew it.

That was, in fact the end of that Revolution!

QUEEN MARIA PIA OF SAVOY

KING CHARLES II OF SPAIN

KING CHARLES II OF SPAIN
d. 1700

Charles II the last, tragic Spanish Habsburg could sire no children.

Throughout his life therefore he had to endure the sight of all Europe quarrelling over his succession and planning to carve up his Empire.

Perhaps he would like to have left his innumerable crowns to his Cousins the Austrian Habsburgs.

In the end, however, he gave in to the ceaseless harrying by the champions of France and left them to the Duke of Anjou, grandson of Louis XIV.

This much-contested decision sparked the War of the Spanish succession which lasted fourteen years.

Charles II of Spain gave an Amethyst topped with a crown of gold and emeralds to his Cousin, Emperor Leopold I.

In the 17th Century an Amethyst was a precious stone of great rarity.

It is believed to bring a love which is spiritual as well as passionate.

The Egyptians used it in their great discs of light which were applied for all diseases of the nerves, pain of nervous origin and to induce calm to a disordered heart.

In "The Devotions of the Roman Church" it is written that the wedding-ring of the Virgin Mary and Joseph was of amethyst.

Charles II was certainly using the Amethyst he gave to Leopold I as a token of affection.

The ties between the Courts of Madrid and Vienna were close, because two branches of the same family had reigned for over a hundred years, since the time of Emperor Charles V.

However, Charles II of Spain died a broken man in 1700.

He could never reconcile himself to the fact that because he had no son, the wrangling and quarrels between his relatives would continue after he was no longer with them.

It was a sad end to a life which should have been a happy and contented one.

KING LOUIS XIV OF FRANCE
1638-1715

King Louis XIV was the most dedicated collector in 17th Century Europe.

He enlarged that begun by Francis I and made it the First Collection of the world.

He bought 9,785 pearls from the Queen of Poland, 45 large diamonds, and 1,122 small ones from Tavernier, 14 large and 131 small from another Jeweller and went on buying until the end of his long reign.

Snatching up everything he could find, the King displayed the Collector's most indispensable quality – greed!

He bought for a low price the diamonds of his Aunt, Queen Henrietta Maria of England when she was in exile, and whom he maintained in the most miserable poverty.

He gave his mistress, *Madame* de Montespan the 'Hope Diamond' as a present.

This gem was also known as the 'Blue Terror' and almost as soon as *Madame* de Montespan received it she lost all favour with her Royal lover.

It was a stone of ill-fortune too for Marie Antoinette.

Then the stone was stolen with the rest of the French Regalia.

In about 1830 a blue diamond was offered for sale in London and was purchased by Henry Philip Hope and was thereafter known as the 'Hope Diamond'.

It is believed by gem experts to have been recut from the 'Blue Terror' or the 'French Blue', as it was known more popularly at that time.

It is noted for its long history and deepening greenish-blue colour.

It was discovered at the Kollar Mines and bought by Tavernier in 1642, after which his fortunes began to change until he died an unhappy man.

According to legend, this stone was originally the eye of a Hindu idol and was plucked out by robbers.

A dozen violent deaths and disasters in two Royal Families are linked to the possession of the Hope Diamond, and have upheld its reputation.

When Louis XIV felt he was nearing death, he decided to put on a show for his Court and the world.

He used as an excuse an audience with the Persian Ambassador to have such an enormous number of diamonds and pearls sewn onto his clothes that he staggered under their weight.

Seventy years after the death of King Louis XIV there was a Revolution in France which resulted in King Louis XVI and his wife Marie Antoinette being imprisoned and eventually going to the guillotine.

During the night of the 15th September, 1792 when Paris was in the throes of the 'September Massacres' a patrol was hurrying across the Place de la Concorde.

The Officer leading the patrol noticed a strange shadow cast by one of the four street lamps.

Looking up he saw a man straddling the iron bracket.

Threatened with soldiers' rifles, the acrobat slithered down, and without hesitation, told his story.

He was part of a band of robbers who had climbed a lamp-post, vaulted onto the balcony of the Garde Meubles, broken through a window and made off with the Crown Jewels.

The Officer and soldiers were horror-struck. They entered the Garde Meubles and found it deserted. None of the 8,000 diamonds of the Crown were left.

The burglars had taken their time, returned night after night, and even paused to picnic on sausage and wine.

They were so laden with booty that they had dropped precious stones all over the Place de la Concorde.

After a desperate search, about 1,500 diamonds were recovered, amongst them such famous ones as the 'Regent' and the 'Sancy'.

Others, including several stones known all over the world, are still at large.

The French Revolution dealt a death-blow to European Monarchies, to their sacred character and to their very meaning.

The concept of the Crown Jewels was to bear the consequences of the change.

In the Middle Ages they had been surrounded by mystique.

They were mere collections after the Renaissance. Altered by the fashions of the 18th century, they fell into vanity in the 19th.

Napoleon the successor, as well as the victor of the revolution made himself Emperor.

Obviously thinking of Charlemagne, he summoned the Pope to crown him and he ordered that the crown be made a simple affair of gilded silver set with modest cameos.

Napoleon first crowned himself with a gold crown of laurels, making an oath to hold undivided all the territories of the Republic.

He repeated the ceremony in Milan for which he ordered a new set of Crown Jewels when crowned King of Italy.

He then started making Kings of his brothers, his brothers-in-law, and promoting the representatives of the oldest dynasties of Germany, counting on the legendary vanity of the German Princes.

Bavaria, Saxony and Wurtemberg became Kingdoms.

Prussia had had one King a century before, when the Holy Roman Emperor Leopold I, needing the Armies of the Elector of Brandenburg to fight Louis XIV, and having nothing in exchange, hit upon the idea of making him King in 1700.

Wild with happiness, Frederick I had ordered a superb crown, ran to Konigsberg to become King of Prussia, and became the Emperor's faithful ally.

KING LOUIS XIV OF FRANCE

QUEEN MARY I OF ENGLAND
1516-1558

Princess Mary was the daughter of Henry VIII and Catherine of Aragon.

When she was two years old, her marriage took place with the baby Dauphin of France, son of Francis I.

The Princess wore on her finger the smallest known diamond ring which was placed there by Cardinal Wolsey, who performed the ceremony.

The bride's gown was of cloth of gold, and her black velvet cap sparkled with jewels.

Unfortunately, the Dauphin died in infancy.

The Princess became Queen of England in 1553 when she was thirty-seven years of age.

She was a strenuous Roman Catholic, and entirely reversed the Religious Order during her brief reign of five years.

Persecuting, imprisoning and burning at the stake Protestant reformers, nearly three-hundred persons were put to death as heretics.

This earned her, and deservedly so, the title of 'Bloody Mary'.

Queen Mary married King Philip of Spain in 1554 when she was thirty-eight.

The Queen was unable to have children and on her death her place on the throne was taken by her half-sister, a Protestant.

Queen Mary's mother was Catherine of Aragon and Elizabeth's was Anne Boleyn, who was beheaded in 1536 on a charge of adultery.

QUEEN MARY I OF ENGLAND

THE EMPRESS JOSEPHINE
1763-1814

Napoleon was crowned Emperor on December 2nd, 1804.

He was anointed by the Pope and he turned to find that his sisters, who carried Josephine's train but who hated her, were making it difficult for her to move towards him.

Josephine was wearing a glittering diamond tiara on her classically-shaped head and round her neck a row of magnificent diamonds to correspond.

There were also diamonds to decorate the basque of her gown.

Napoleon's manner of crowning Josephine was in itself remarkable.

After lifting up the crown surmounted by a cross, he had put it first on his head, then transferred it to the Empress's.

His manner was almost playful.

He put the crown on, then took it off, then finally put it on again as if to promise Josephine that she would wear it gracefully and lightly for ever.

It was a day of triumph for her because she had fought against the Emperor's whole family who were furious when they realised that he had married her.

His courtship had been very ardent as he had fallen madly in love.

They had slept together because Josephine was perfectly prepared to accept him as a lover, while she could not make up her mind as the widow of Alexander de Beauharnais to actually marry someone who was not considered by the French to have 'blue blood.'

In fact, she was well aware that they called Napoleon sneakingly the 'Corsican Corporal.'

He wrote to her after their first night of love:

". . . my waking thoughts are all of you, your portrait and remembrance of last night's delirium have robbed

*my sense of repose. Sweet and incomparable Josephine,
what an extraordinary influence you have on my heart!
Are you vexed? Did I see you frown? Are you ill at ease?
My soul is broken with grief and there is no rest for your
lover. But is there more for me when, delivering ourselves
up to the deep feelings which master me, I breathe out
upon your lips, upon your heart, a flame which burns
me up? Ah! it was this past night I realised that your
portrait was not you.*

*You start at noon . . . I shall see you in three hours.
Meanwhile, nio dolce amor, accept a thousand kisses,
but give me none, for they fire my blood."*

They were finally married in a very strange way one
stormy night.

On Wednesday 8th March, 1796 the Mayor of the district
in which Napoleon lived was got out of bed and told to
perform a Marriage Ceremony immediately.

The simple civil ceremony provided under the
Revolutionary régime was soon over.

The bride and groom returned to Josephine's house, to
the same bed where in the past few weeks they had already
found happiness.

They were not married for long before Napoleon became
suspicious and very jealous of Josephine.

He wrote to her in May, 1796:

*"My life is a perpetual nightmare as a presentiment of
fear approaches me. I see you no longer. I have lost more
than life, more than happiness, I am almost without
hope."*

In June he wrote;

*"A thousand kisses on your eyes, your lips, your tongue,
your heart. Most charming of your sex, what is your
power over me? I am still very ill of your illness. I still
have burning fever, Do not keep the courier more than
six hours. Let him return at once to bring the longed-
for letter from my beloved."*

At the end of June his letter was more intense because
he had not heard from her.

"I warn you, you have made me miserable. Cruel one! Why have you led me to place hope in a feeling which you do not possess? Is life worth making so much fuss about? Adieu, Josephine, remain in Paris. Do not write me any more. But at least respect my hearth. A thousand daggers tear my soul. Do not drive them any further. Adieu, my happiness, my love, everything that has existed for me on earth!"

The storm broke when Josephine was in Milan, engrossed with her lover Hippolyte Charles.

Napoleon wrote to her in November, 1769:

"What inclination stifles and alienates love? The affectionate and unvarying love which you promised me? Who may this paragon be, this new lover who engrosses all your time, is master of your days, and prevents you from concerning yourself about your husband? Josephine, be vigilant; one fine night the doors will be broken in, and I shall be before you."

Josephine went too far and finally Napoleon listened to his brother Lucien and decided he would have nothing more to do with her.

Lucien told him over and over again that he must be firm and divorce her.

Napoleon agreed, but "When she begs and prays you will forgive her," he said sarcastically.

"I forgive her?" Napoleon answered. "Never? You know me well. If I was not sure of my own feelings I would tear my heart out and throw it into the fire."

Uttering these words Napoleon seemed to be nearly choking with rage.

He clutched at his breast as if he would tear it open.

Lucien departed, and before he left Bonaparte invited him to breakfast in the morning.

In the meantime. Josephine, who had gone to meet her husband on his way home, but missed him, returned to the house.

She discovered that Napoleon neither wished to see her nor speak to her.

His anger had not grown calmer, but merely increased. "Never, never again will I take her back!"

As he said these words he shut himself up in his Study and began to pace up and down the room in his agitation.

Josephine, dishevelled and tired, knocked on the door.

"Open the door, *mon amor*. You pain me. I will explain everything."

Her voice was broken with her deep sobs.

"Oh, you will not open the door. Why are you so angry with me?"

She cried out that she loved him.

Her heart-broken sobs would have softened the heart of a statue.

But Napoleon was unmoved, and paid no attention to her pleas.

Now, her prayers were replaced by despair and supplication, but it had no effect upon the heart which hitherto had been hers.

Josephine passed a terrible night.

She lay down on the floor weeping bitterly outside the closed door behind which was the man she had despised.

Whose honour she had dragged in the mud while he was away exposed to countless dangers.

The man she had covered with ridicule, if such a genius could have been made ridiculous by such a silly creature.

Now she lay there, only half clothed, over-whelmed by despair, a picture of grief, begging pardon of him whom she had wounded so cruelly.

Then her waiting woman told her to send her children to the General.

Josphine immediately saw the wisdom of this.

It was evident the Gereral knew all about her misconduct he would no longer love the woman who had shown him so clearly she did not love him.

Besides which, she had trifled so much with his honour for her to dare to appeal to his affection.

But she still possessed one weapon and a very powerful one.

She still had her children and she could make use of their tears and their pleas.

Napoleon had always been very fond of young Eugene, whom he thought was brave.

In fact he loved him.

He was also fond of Hortense, who, although so young, promised to become a good and clever woman.

He had actually loved and cared for the young people as if they were his own children.

Josephine felt he could not find it in his heart to say to them: "Go with your mother? I do not want anything more to do with her. She is exceedingly cruel and she does not even deserve to be hated! She only deserves to be despised."

Could he say that?

No — the Napoleon she knew could never tell those weeping children that their mother was a despicable creature.

She hurried off to fetch her son and daughter.

No one had slept in the house in the Rue de la Victoire that night.

She briefly told them what she wanted them to do — what they *must* do.

She had guessed right.

How could he tell the young people that their mother had been guilty of misconduct?

Napoleon was obliged, despite his fury to be silent.

His anger melted away at the sight of those poor, young innocent creatures who knelt at his feet, covering their eyes with their hands and crying:

"Do not desert our mother: it will kill her! And what shall we do if we lose you, whom God has sent to defend us?"

Napoleon looked at these poor orphans, whose father had already been devoured by the guillotine.

The man who had vanquished both Austria and Turkey, was vanquished in turn by the defenceless young children.

"Very well," he said, "go and fetch your mother."

The two children ran and found her lying rent with grief on the stairs leading to the servants' quarters.

Her despair was genuine.

"Mama — come!" they cried. "The General is waiting for you."

She ran into his arms, neither of them able to speak a single word.

Her tears were choking her, and then she fainted.

Napoleon picked her up in his arms.

When Lucien called to see his brother the following morning, it was to find them lying side by side.

It was no wonder that as Napoleon crowned Josephine his Empress she felt as if he also crowned her heart.

THE EMPRESS JOSEPHINE

MAHARAJAH KHANDE RAO, GAEKWAR OF BARODA

THE MAHARAJAH KHANDE RAO, GAEKWAR OF BARODA

The Gaekwar of Baroda had precedence over all the Rulers in India at all functions.

He governed a Province of about 8,225 square miles in the Western part of India 248 miles North of Bombay.

His treasures were estimated at $12 million and had been collected by his predecessors who lived in barbaric splendour.

The treasures included a sash of a hundred rows of pearls, terminating in a great tassel of pearls and emeralds; seven rows of superb pearls whose value is estimated at half a million dollars; a litter set with seed-pearls, quantities of unstrung pearls, and more remarkable, a shawl or carpet of pearls.

The carpet is said to be 10½ feet long by six feet wide, and to made up of strings of pearls.

There is a border 11″ wide and also the centre ornaments worked in diamonds.

It is believed that this fantastic ornament was originally intended as a covering for the tomb of Mohammed.

Over 670 Princes or independent Chiefs were recognised by the British, but the principle by which the British distinguished the greater Princes from the smaller was the allotment of gun salutes.

About a hundred could be greeted on formal occasions by the thunder of nine or more guns, and they were also entitled to be addressed as 'Your Highness'.

The Maharajah Khande Rao whose reign lasted from 1856 to 1870 was very eccentric.

Everything he took a fancy to he had to have at once.

One day he demanded big diamonds; another day he chose religion.

On this occasion he collected a Holy Man who was sitting in a trance on a dunghill.

He was brought to the Palace and surrounded with

Sadhus, but they learnt nothing, not even when a pistol was fired near the Holy Man's ear.

On another occasion Khande Rao demanded 60,000 pigeons of all different species.

He had his priests conduct a marriage ceremony over a pair of them, and gave a vast banquet with fireworks.

But he lost interest when one of the Palace cats carried off the bridegroom.

He then decided to organise a battle between five-hundred nightingales.

Some of the Maharajah's entertainments were more vigorous.

Baroda was famous for its arena where, echoing Imperial Rome, beasts and men were matched.

It was three hundred yards long and two hundred yards wide, and was enclosed by twenty-two foot walls painted in a startling candy pink.

Outside in the grounds around the Palace a solitary bull might be teased by men with spears and fire-crackers, waving red veils, or by horsemen with a lance.

At other times a fight would be arranged between rams and buffaloes charging at each other until they could no longer move.

But the only event that sometimes ended with a death was the wresting.

In Baroda men fought with claws of sharpened horn lashed to their wrists.

Drunk with liquid opium and hemp, they became oblivious to pain: a loser might be literally torn to strips before he was carried from the arena.

The winner received money from the Maharajah and perhaps a rope of pearls and a silk coat of honour.

On a single day Khande Rao might distribute four thousand pounds worth of such prizes.

His own jewels were fantastic.

In 1867 he paid sixty thousand pounds for the Star of the South, the first diamond of any size and reputed to be taken from the newly developed Brazilian mines.

It was also the largest diamond ever found by a woman. She was an African slave.

Her reward was her freedom and a pension for life.

When the stone arrived in Baroda, Khande Rao gave a triumphal parade graced by a saddled and bridled giraffe.

The Maharajah then placed the diamond in a necklace with another stone.

This was a pear-shaped diamond of such purity that when the Koh-i-noor was tested beside it, it made that famous jewel seem slightly yellow.

It had cost Khande Rao thirty-thousand pounds.

He had paid twenty-five thousand less for the Akbar Shah, a tear-drop diamond of 70 carats which was believed to have been one of the eyes of the peacock on the Peacock Throne of the Monguls.

His novel method of disposing of opponents set new standards in sadism.

He would strap a man to the hind leg of an elephant, give the beast a sharp prod to make it move at a fast pace, dragging the victim along with it.

If the victim was merely concussed he would be revived by throwing water over him, then his head would be placed on a large stone and the elephant was encouraged to step on it.

Khande Rao was deposed by the British after he had stood trial for the attempted murder of a Colonial Chief.

KING RICHARD I

RICHARD I
RICHARD THE LION-HEARTED
1157-99

King of England from 1189 to his death.

He laid heavy burdens upon the people in order to equip an Army for the third Crusade.

At first he was victorious and did such valiant deeds that he received the name of *'Coeur de Lion'*.

Being ultimately defeated, he signed a truce with Saladin, and on his way back to England was shipwrecked.

Disguised as a pilgrim, he was identified in Austria, and handed over to the Emperor of Germany, who imprisoned him in a remote castle.

A large sum was demanded and paid for his ransom, and after over a year of durance he returned to England and was crowned at Winchester.

During the reign of the eighth-century Sultan Abd-er-Rahman in Moorish Spain, fifty young and idealistic Noblemen formed a bodyguard for the Sultan, vowing eternal loyalty to each other and eternal fidelity each to his own chosen woman.

As an elite body they ordered richly decorated armour and remembered a legend about carbuncles.

Once upon a time, there was a mine in Persia which produced unusually large red carbuncles of a heart shape and imbedded in iron ore. It was soon noted that those who carried the carbuncles in their rough state were very lucky in love, but for those who mounted them in gold, the stones did nothing.

Because the magic was not impaired when the stones were worn in iron rings or on the steel of breastplates and helmets, the carbuncles were sent to Toledo in Spain and there inserted in the armour for which that city was famous.

Every wealthy Moorish warrior was eager to own the carbuncles, which were called the "loadstones of love," but time revealed a serious disadvantage to this love amulet. It was death to unfaithful lovers.

The young Noblemen searched through old lumber rooms and cellars until they had enough carbuncles to stud their helmets, their collars, and their chain mail which extended from shoulder to thigh.

When the Moors invaded France in 732 this glorious company led the Army mounted on prancing horses and glittering in their bejewelled armour.

As the noble young Knights advanced through enemy country, the splendour of their appearance gradually diminished.

Centuries later, when King Richard was engaged in a war with France, a rumour was circulated that a peasant ploughing the fields of Limousin in the centre of the country near the Castle of Challus had fallen into a subterranean cavern and found a curious treasure.

On a table heaped with jewels and golden plate sat twelve life-size figures made of gold.

In accordance with feudal law, Aimer of Limoges claimed the treasure from Achard of Chalus who was reported to have it in his keeping.

Richard, the Lion-Hearted, however, as King of England, Duke of Aquitane and Normandy and Count of Anjou, had the superior claim and demanded his rights.

Achard replied that nothing had been found except a few suits of rusted armour containing human bones.

King Richard in a rage, besieged the Castle of Chalus.

Achard sent a suit of antique armour to the King as proof that nothing of value was to be had.

On the shoulders and belt of the dingy armour gleamed red carbuncles.

Richard, thinking his vassal a liar and a traitor donned the ancient armour and swore that clad in this miserable evidence of disloyalty he would capture the Castle and hang the defenders.

As the King approached the Castle walls, the rusted shoulder clasp broke and a bolt from a crossbow inflicted a deep wound.

He fought on for ten days until the Castle surrendered, but by then a severe infection of the wound prevented him doing any more.

Before he died, his wife, Berengaria of Navarre, from whom he was estranged and to whom he had not been faithful arrived for a reconciliation.

She had been deeply moved by a strange resurgence of love for her husband and a foreboding of disaster.

King Richard's death was a blow for England.

What was to be remembered in the future was that his bravery and valiant deeds had crowned him for ever with the name of *'Coeur de Lion'*.

QUEEN ELEANOR OF FRANCE

QUEEN ELEANOR OF FRANCE

In 1530 François I, King of France, married for the second time.

It was a politically arranged marriage and the bride was Eleanor of Austria.

Sister of the Emperor Charles V, she had briefly been the third wife of King Manoel of Portugal, who had died in 1521.

Eleanor was Flemish and born in 1498 — attractive, but quiet, shy and self-effacing — she was not the right person to cope with the wildly attractive King.

Every woman he met succumbed to his charm. He also had a vibrant brain and was irresistibly attracted to women, as they were to him.

Eleanor arrived in France in June 1530 and was married the next month at a little Convent near Villeneauve-de-Marsin.

The next year, on March 5th, she was crowned Queen of France at St. Denis. The diamonds, emeralds and rubies she wore were worth more than a million gold crowns.

However, it was known later that when the new Queen was undressed, her body was so long that she seemed to have the trunk of a giant.

Yet so short were her legs and thighs that she might have been a dwarf!

The Court took little notice of her.

When the Queen made her ceremonial entry into Paris in March 1531, the King with his mistress, Anne d'Heilly, sat side by side in sight of all the people in a window for two hours watching, talking and laughing.

Eleanor however had her jewels. Hers were more fantastic than any her husband's mistress could afford.

Her caps were sewn with jewels and pearls and stones of enormous value were sewn onto the bodice of her gown and her large puffed sleeves.

KING ARTHUR

KING ARTHUR
c. 6th Century

Arthur was a famous British Chieftain and later King who flourished in the 6th Century.

Many beautiful legends have been written about his life and Court.

One day, Arthur went to a glen in Lyonnesse and came upon the bodies of two brothers who had met in combat.

One of the corpses wore a crown of diamonds which Arthur picked up.

Once he became King, Arthur helped to rebuild towns and restore order.

Among the lesser Kings whom Arthur helped was King Leodegrance of Cameliard.

He had a beautiful daughter called Guenevere, and Arthur fell in love with her at first sight.

Guenevere's father consented to their wedding because he loved the good and knightly King.

With great pomp, the Princess was conducted to Canterbury, where the King awaited her. They were wed by the Archbishop in the Cathedral.

King Leodegrance's wedding gift to Arthur was a round table and on the day of his wedding Arthur founded his Order of the Round Table.

One hundred and fifty Knights could sit round it.

King Arthur knighted one hundred and twenty-eight at his wedding feast.

He also offered nine diamonds from the crown he had found, as the prize of nine several jousts — 'one every year, a joust for one!'

Lancelot, having won eight, intended when they were all won, to present them to the Queen.

But when he laid them before her, a lady in love with him, in a fit of jealousy snatched them up and flung them out of the Palace window into the river below.

King Arthur held his realm in peace, doing justice to all.

EMPRESS CATHERINE THE GREAT

CATHERINE THE GREAT – EMPRESS OF RUSSIA
1729-1796

The daughter of a Prussian General, Catherine married in 1775 when she was twenty-one the future Tzar Peter III of Russia.

All Europe was scandalised by the Empress.

She announced in July 1762 that her Coronation would take place in September.

Catherine's lover, Gregory Orloff had helped her to seize power through a *coup d'etat*.

With his own hands it was said he had killed her husband, who was a weakling and something of an embarrassment.

Catherine's next announcement therefore was that her husband had died suddenly of colic but no one believed this improbable tale.

The Foreign Embassies were soon buzzing with the story as to how the Tzar had really met his death.

Nobody knows exactly what happened: some said he was poisoned and strangled with a table napkin.

But his face was black and his body badly bruised.

They whispered that Catherine was not only a murderess but a usurper, and not only a usurper, but a whore.

That a German Princess of petty origin should have snatched the crown first from her husband, then from her son Paul was bad enough.

But she was also pregnant with her lover's child.

Catherine however appeared oblivious of what anyone said, either in Russia, or abroad.

On the day of her Coronation she made Gregory Orloff her Adjutant General, gave him the title of Count and presented him with her portrait set in diamonds.

This he wore over his heart.

She installed him in the Winter Palace in rooms which had a private staircase leading up to her own apartment.

The Princess Dashkova who was one of those in the

conspiracy to place the Empress on the throne describes in her diaries how she had seen count Orloff sprawling on the sofa in the Empress's Drawing-Room opening Official Communications.

The French Charge d'Affaires reported:

"He lacks nothing but the title of Emperor . . . scorning etiquette, he takes liberties with his Sovereign in public which in polished society no self-respecting mistress permits in her lover."

In private Count Orloff beat Catherine and she fell more deeply in love with what she described as 'The most handsome man I have ever known.'

She did, however, remain sensible enough to resist his constant plea that they should be married.

She undoubtedly toyed with the idea, but her Chancellor pointed out that an upstart like Orloff who had fathered her child, Count Alexis Bobrinsky would be a threat to the legitimate heir and would cause opposition.

"Madame Orloff," he told her, "could never remain Empress of Russia."

With difficulty, Catherine managed to ignore Orloff's tirades and although she wept because he punished her by being unfaithful, she continued to shower him with riches.

At this time Catherine was tall and slender, but as her French Secretary said, she was not very subtle.

"She has a noble carriage," he said, "an affected and somewhat ungraceful walk, with a narrow chest, a long face, especially about the chin, an eternal smile on her lips, a deep-set mouth, a slightly aquiline nose, small eyes, an agreeable expression, and a face marked by smallpox."

Catherine believed that opulence went with power.

If foreigners were impressed by the luxury of Elizabeth's reign, they were also impressed by her as an Empress.

"The richness and splendour of the Russian Court surpasses all description," wrote a Visitor, "and her bodyguard is the most sumptuously dressed in Europe."

In Catherine's Court the men outshone the ladies at night in the use of precious stones.

"Count Orloff sported a suit in which was sewn a million-pounds worth of diamonds," and the British Minister, Sir James Harris, described a fête at which "the dessert at supper was set out with jewels to the amount of upwards of two million sterling."

Catherine's love of grandeur however was not limited to personal splendour.

She began to build in St. Petersburg a magnificent noble Palace for Gregory Orloff and added three buildings to the immense Winter Palace which already boasted 1,500 rooms.

Catherine then discovered that Gregory Orloff was having an affair with the Princess Golitsyna and decided that the time had come to end the liaison.

Orloff was astonished. It was something he had never expected and he could not believe that she was really serious.

Catherine was hysterical in her longing for him and wrote:

"All the caresses provoke nothing in me but tears so that I believe I have never cried since my birth as I have in these last eighteen months. I thought at first I would get accustomed to the situation, but things grew worse and worse."

However, Catherine was determined not to have her old lover back.

When Orloff learnt that Alexander Vasilchikov was living in his apartment he was wild with rage and set out to St. Petersburg without a moment's delay.

On Catherine's orders he was stopped and confined to his Palace some distance outside the capital.

Catherine was so frightened of him that she changed all the locks on the Palace doors and kept an armed guard outside her rooms.

"You do not know him," she wailed, "he is capable of killing me, and of killing the Grand Duke."

In the end, Orloff regained his composure and was allowed to return, not only to St. Petersburg, but to the

Winter Palace.

In the Winter Palace Catherine loaded him with gifts: six thousand serfs, a salary of 150,000 roubles, a service of Sèvres china, porcelain worth 250,000 roubles.

In return he gave Catherine a superb solitaire diamond which cost him 460,000 roubles.

The 'Orloff Diamond'', as it came to be called, had a fascinating history.

In the eighteenth century a deserter from the French Army visited the Temple near Trichinapoly in Mysore, where he saw an enormous diamond set as an 'eye' in a statue of Brahma.

The soldier pretended to be an ardent convert to Hinduism and begged to be allowed to spend the night in the Temple, in order to 'better pray to Brahma.'

He then prised out one of the idol's eyes and absconded with it.

In London he sold it to a Jewish merchant and soon afterwards it was offered to Catherine, who refused it, thinking the price was excessive.

However, Gregory Orloff bought it and thought it would be a way of getting back into Catherine's favour.

She accepted the diamond, but did not reinstate him.

She never wore the 200 carat diamond, but had it set in her sceptre.

It was, however, to be a jewel of ill-omen to Russia, particularly Tzar Nicholas II, the last of the Romanovs.

Today, the Orloff Diamond is in the Kremlin.

KING ALEXANDER THE GREAT
356-323 B.C.

Alexander was a restless, energetic, fearless, headstrong, self-willed boy. His self-will came from an intelligent, inventive independence.

When he was twelve years old, Philonicus of Thessaly offered to sell King Philip, his father, his horse Bucephalus for thirteen talents.

They all went down to the plain to see the animal which proved, to be very restless. He would not let anyone mount him. None of the King's attendants could do anything with him either.

The King, therefore, ordered the horse to be led away as being utterly wild and untrained.

Hearing this Alexander said:

"That is too good a horse for those men to spoil simply because they haven't the skill or the grit to handle him."

At first King Philip paid no attention to his son, but as he insisted on being heard, his father said to him:

"What do you mean by criticising your elders, as if you were wiser than they, or knew more about handling a horse then they do?"

"I could handle the horse better than anyone else," replied Alexander, "if they would give me a chance."

On hearing this, his father asked him what penalty he would pay if he failed.

"I'll pay, by Jove, the price of the horse!" Alexander retorted.

This was greeted with laughter from the people standing around, but Alexander went to the horse, took him by the bridle and turned him round towards the sun.

He knew that the horse's fright was due to seeing his own shadow dance up and down on the ground before him.

He then ran beside him for a while, patting and coaxing him, then seeing the animal was impatient to go, he threw off his coat and swung himself on the saddle.

Alexander then rode the horse fully until he let him go,

driving him on. The group of onlookers were concerned, until as the boy turned the horse and galloped back to them with pride and joy on his face, they burst into cheers.

When Alexander dismounted, the father kissed him, saying:

"My son, seek thee a kingdom suited to thy powers: Macedonia is too strait for thee."

Alexander grew up and as a youth enjoyed athletics and gymnastics, and was known to be "swift of feet." He also enjoyed ball games and mounting and dismounting from a chariot at full speed.

His education also included mathematics, natural history, medicine and literature. He enjoyed Homer's Illiad, and had instruction in physiology and botany.

Alexander from the very first showed himself to be fitted for mighty military exploits.

He conquered in turn the Thebans, the Persian Satraps, overthrew Darius and overran Syria and Phoenicia.

He possessed himself of all the Cities along the Mediterranean, conquered Egypt and founded Alexandria.

After thinking of the scheme for the City, he proceeded to mark out the plan, including the sites for market-places, streets, public buildings, temples of the different deities, each of which was specially assigned.

The basis of the plan was two main streets crossing each other at right angles, each one hundred feet wide, and lined with colonnades.

Other streets, running parallel to these, were laid out in squares, covering a length of about three miles and a width of about one.

Excavations conducted in 1867 found the plan essentially as described, with in the centre of these avenues, a pavement of grey granite blocks forty-six feet wide as a carriage-way.

The private houses were low, flat-roofed and of stone. Near the centre of the City were the Royal buildings, which occupied, with their gardens, a quarter of the city's area.

While the King was congratulating himself on his plan, a flock of birds flew over the land settling upon the spot where the city was to be, devouring all the flour.

Alexander was disturbed by this, taking it as an ill-omen, until he was assured that the City was destined to be rich in its resources, and a feeder of the nations of men.

It is thought Alexander often drank an excess of wine, but he was not so much addicted to it, but enjoyed spending a long time at the table, conversing, and with each cup he would start a special topic for prolonged conversation and discussion.

Alexander's parents, feared that their son was sexually impotent, and decided to give him a beautiful Thessalian Courtesan called Callixene, hoping she would attract him. Callixene however, had to beg Alexander to give her a little attention.

At the age of thirty-three Alexander, after a very busy life, retired to Babylon, where he died eleven days later.

It is believed that Alexander gave his soldiers lodestones as a defence against the wiles of evil spirits.

The Lodestone is of black iron ore of great magnetism.

A legend of the old Phoenician mariners tells that Hercules, admiring their daring and skill, wanted to help them in the science of navigation.

He obtained a cupful of Lodeston which always turned to the North, which would seem to indicate that the mariners' compass is older than is generally believed.

The Lodestone is also a love amulet with magnetic powers over emotional problems and diseases and had been called "The Stone that Shows the Way".

It was believed that a piece of Lodestone, placed beneath the pillow of a sleeping wife, would act as a touchstone of her virtue.

KING ALEXANDER THE GREAT

QUEEN ELIZABETH OF ENGLAND
1533-1603

Queen Elizabeth of England came to the throne of England in 1558 at the age of twenty-five and reigned for forty-five years.

She was a fervent Protestant and a sincere lover of her country.

She was a masterful and enlightened Ruler, fickle as far as her favourites were concerned.

The Queen added distinction to a distinctive period.

The defeat of the Spanish Armada, the execution of Mary Stuart, the Naval supremacy of England, the extension of her Colonies.

These, as well as the glory of a great new literature of which Shakespeare was the brightest ornament are features associated with her reign.

One of the most romantic, but tragic stories about Elizabeth is that of her love for the Earl of Essex.

She gave him a ring containing a Sardonyx, carved with her portrait 'in token of esteem' with the intimation that if ever he forfeited her favour, and it should be sent back to her, the sight of it would ensure forgiveness.

When Essex lay under sentence of death, he decided to send the ring to her in the hope that she would remember her promise.

He knew however, that he was surrounded by enemies and rather than trust any of his attendants, he looked out of his window and saw a boy whom he induced by a bribe to carry the ring, which he threw down to him, to his Cousin, Lady Scrope.

The boy, by mistake, took the ring to the Countess of Nottingham, her cruel sister, who carried it to the Lord Admiral, a deadly foe of Essex.

The Queen waited, hoping for the token to arrive, and when it did not concluded that Essex was to proud to appeal to her.

She waited in vain and sadly the execution took place.

Years later the Queen visited the Countess of Nottingham on her death-bed who confessed what she had done.

Queen Elizabeth cried out bitterly:

"God may forgive you, but I cannot!'

She died three days after the Countess of Nottingham on the 28th February 1603.

QUEEN ELIZABETH I

KING AUGUSTUS OF SAXONY

H.R.H. KING AUGUSTUS OF SAXONY

Augustus the Strong became King of Saxony in April 1694.

Of all the Monarchs of the Baroque period, none was the equal of Augustus.

He was tall with thick black eyebrows and dark eyes and his physical strength was fantastic.

To impress his dinner guests, he would pick up two of his State trumpeters, one in each hand, and hold them at arms' length for five minutes while they played a fanfare.

He kept a harem of beautiful women and when he died he left 354 bastards. It was so difficult for him to keep track of his love-children, that at least two of his daughters subsequently became his mistresses.

He was able to eat and drink without getting fat and was called "The Ever-Cheerful Man of Sin", and "Gay eupeptic Son of Belial".

Augustus awarded himself the 'Emerald Order of the White Eagle', a Polish Order, upon being elected King of Poland in 1697.

It did not prevent him from losing and regaining his throne three times.

The largest green diamond in the world, known as 'The Green Diamond of Dresden' once belonged to one of his sons.

It escaped the bombing of Dresden in the Second World War and is now locked safely in a vault in that City.

Augustus's son was even more interested in pictures than power and his passion for the arts was even greater than his father's.

But though he adored beauty he fell madly in love with the clever, fascinating – but excessively plain, almost dwarfish – Archduchess Maria Josepha, and married her in 1719 in Vienna.

When the happy pair arrived in Dresden, his father mistook a very pretty Lady-in-Waiting for the bride and kissed her with paternal fervour.

After the mistake had been pointed out to him, Augustus the Strong consoled the pretty Lady-in-Waiting for not being his daughter-in-law by making her his mistress.

QUEEN CATHERINE OF ARAGON
1485-1536

It was at the Field of Cloth of Gold with its glory, its glitter and its luxury that King Henry VIII became restless.

He had not realised until then that Queen Catherine was looking very old.

She came from Spain where the women aged early and now at thirty-five she was saddened and embittered by the knowledge that she had been unable to give her husband what he so greatly desired, a son.

Henry VIII on the other hand, at twenty-nine was in the prime of life.

He was large, very strong and exceedingly good-looking.

He was an accomplished musician and composed some of his own music.

He was a wrestler, he spoke good French, Latin and Spanish and he was exceedingly athletic.

He hunted, if he could, five days a week and would tire eight to ten horses in a day.

Each was stationed beforehand along the line of the country over which he intended the chase to go.

Then as soon as one was tired, he mounted another and while he returned home in good shape, all his horses were exhausted!

He was a good tennis player and his friends and Courtiers found him amusing and very intelligent.

It was not surprising that the Queen loved her English King with a fierce and jealous affection.

The daughter of King Ferdinand and Queen Isabella of Spain, she always remained in heart and in policy a Spanish Princess.

The King, having been faithful to his wife ever since they married fell in love with Elizabeth Blount.

She bore him a son who was given the name of Henry Fitzroy.

Later he became the Duke of Buckingham and the King

played with the idea of making him his heir.

Where Queen Catherine was concerned, the writing was on the wall.

She owned a ruby ring and it was believed that for a ruby to change its colour was a forerunner to misfortune.

The Queen, seeing a change in her ring, was saddened in her heart because she knew it foretold her downfall.

This became true.

As the Queen was unable to give her husband a male heir to the throne he attempted to obtain Papal consent to the dissolution of the marriage.

It was refused.

This led to the suppression of the Monasteries and what was known as the Reformation Crisis in England.

QUEEN CATHERINE OF ARAGON

KING JOHN

KING JOHN OF ENGLAND
1167-1216

The most disastrous loss of jewels took place when King John came to the throne of England in 1200.

He loved jewellery and had a famous collection, but it was all lost in the quicksands of the Wash when he was travelling North and the tide came in to sweep away his horses before any could be rescued.

Among the pieces lost was the Regale worn by his grandmother Matilda when she was crowned Empress.

John himself was short, dark and proud.

He was the youngest son of Henry Plantagenet.

He was born when his mother was forty-five and destined for the Church.

At the age of nine he was bethrothed to his second Cousin, Isabella, daughter of the Earl of Gloucester.

His bride failed to bear him any children and the marriage was eventually declared invalid.

He continued to be friendly with her and sent her presents of wine and sugar.

Finally he married her to the Earl of Essex who had to pay 20,000 marks for her.

Then in 1200 John fell passionately in love.

She was Isabelle, daughter of Count Audemar of Angouleme in Aquitaine and she was only twelve years old.

She was already engaged to a widower Hugh IX, Lord of Lusignan and Count of La Marche.

John swept Isabelle into his arms and carried her across the Channel to England, where they were crowned together at Westminster Abbey.

They spent the next six months travelling round England, just as previously he had toured his lands in France.

They spent Easter at Canterbury where they 'wore their crowns,' and Hubert Walter as Archbishop performed the ceremony at the feast.

So furious was Hugh IX that his bride-to-be should have been abducted in such a way that he caused a row that resulted in the ensuing war when King John lost all his possessions.

John and Isabelle had two sons and three daughters, and he also had three illegitimate children.

He spent much of his time hunting, and loved food and wine.

He had an obsession for eggs and ordered five-thousand for his Christmas festivities in 1206.

King John wished to cross The Wash, taking with him many of his most valuable possessions.

Horses and mules travelled behind him laden with baggage, money and, most precious of all, the Royal crown which King John had intended to put away in a safe place.

There was a procession trailing along behind the King's carriage, all having crossed The Wash where the sand was firm and dry.

A great mistake must have been made regarding the times of low and high tide, for they were just in the middle of the sand when back came a high tide.

It swept away everything, goods, money, valuables — all were sucked under in the ensuing whirlpool.

King John however was saved.

When he learned that he had lost all his property he stamped his feet and screamed with passion.

He behaved so violently that his servants would not dare to tell him that the Royal crown was amongst things that were now at the bottom of the sea.

These included a clasp ornamented with emeralds and rubies, four rings, one with an emerald, one with a sapphire, one with garnets and one with a topaz.

There were also a hundred and forty-three cups of white silver and a wand of gold with a cross.

When at last he heard the news he went to bed and refused to eat or drink for several days.

He came so ill that he fancied he had received a warning from Heaven that he would no longer be King.

He ran a fever and this and the loss of his treasure weighed so heavily on his mind that he died in the year 1216, when he was only forty-nine years of age.

SIR BHUPINDER SINGH
THE MAHARAJAH OF PATIALA

His Highness the Maharajah of Patiala wore the jewels he had bought from the Empress Eugénie of France, for £300,000.

He was nearly six feet six inches tall, weighed twenty stone, most of it bone and muscle.

He lived in a pink Palace a quarter-of-a-mile long with rose-red roofs.

White peacocks screamed among its pinnacles, an Afghan staghound might answer from the driveway, or a tiger roar from where it was chained beyond the lotus pools.

There were thiry-five hundred servants in the Maharajah's service, amongst them many cooks.

He ate fifty pounds of food a day, although he always said he ate only one meal.

Three whole chickens might disappear at tea-time and after dinner he left his guests while he helped himself to an immense gold dish of rice and meats and sugary confections with his fingers.

He had five-hundred horses, a large pack of champion gun-dogs and a fleet of cars which included twenty-seven Rolls-Royces.

His suits, which came from Savile Row could be counted in their hundreds, and he kept three-hundred and fifty women in his Harem.

One of the last Princes to be able to exercise absolute power within his own Sect, he once raided across the border.

He was interested in a fair-haired, blue-eyed girl he had noticed while hunting and wanted her.

There was a battle and Bhupinder Singh won against his Cousin Nabha, whose land he had raided and to whom he showed no mercy.

The Maharajah had every comfort in his Palace including a pool filled with great blocks of ice floating on it during the summer which helped to keep the temperature down to a reasonable 60°.

He had frescoes showing the erotic expertise of the Indians.

His Harem was highly organised, and very different from those of his contemporaries.

It contained Beauty Salons, Jewellers, Perfumiers, Dressmakers and Hairdressers.

There were also Indian, French and English Doctors, who were capable of undertaking Plastic Surgery.

One of their most important operations was the reshaping of a woman's breasts to the taste and demands of His Highness.

He indulged in a long study of deodorants, douches, lotions and philtres.

It was not surprising that he needed so much for he had three-hundred and fifty women in his Harem.

There was also a need for aphrodisiacs and His Highness's Indian Doctors tried combinations of pearls and gold, silver, iron, herbs and spices.

They were successful with a concoction of carrots mixed with the brains of the sparrow, which is noted as a lascivious bird.

As their attempts were not particularly successful, however, the French Doctors were called in and consulted.

They recommended a machine containing radium, to 'increase the spermatogenic power and capacity of the testicles and to stimulate the erection centre'.

Actually, the Maharajah was not so concerned with 'spermatogenic power'.

All he was really suffering from was boredom and selfishness.

In March 1938 he lay dying in Patiala as innumerable pigeons cooed in the red apertures of his titanic Palace.

In the tropical foliage of the garden six tall Sikh footmen pushed perambulators containing the babies that had arrived that week.

His dead body, bathed by his gurus according to the Sikh custom was seated for the last time on the throne of Patiala.

It was then carried on a pyre through the City, where more than a million people came to watch it pass.

His last child was born approximately nine months later to one of the women of his Harem.

It was a son.

THE MAHARAJAH OF PATIALA

MARY QUEEN OF SCOTS
1542-1587

Mary Queen of Scots was a Queen from birth and was crowned when she was nine months old.

She was married to the Dauphin of France at sixteen years of age.

On the death of her husband in 1560 she returned to Scotland and for a time was the acknowledged Queen of the Scots.

In 1565 she married Lord Darnley, who was murdered a year later, and Queen Mary then married Bothwell.

Scottish nobles rebelled against her and she was imprisoned in Loch Leven Castle, where she was compelled to abandon Bothwell and to sign an Act of Abdication in favour of her son.

She escaped to England and sought refuge under the protection of her Cousin Queen Elizabeth.

It is doubtful if the Royal Crown of Scotland was actually placed on baby Mary's head.

It was however used by her son James I, and later her grandson Charles I.

This crown incorporates the far older crown of the Stuart ancestors as well as the crown belonging to Robert the Bruce (1274-1329).

Some people consider it a far more elegant crown than the English ones, and it was ordered in the 16th Century by James V of Scotland.

In modern times the crown is merely presented to British Rulers to signify their accession, and is kept in the care of the Dukes of Hamilton.

Mary Queen of Scots was imprisoned in various Castles for nineteen years, and ultimately beheaded on a charge of conspiracy.

Wearing a red gown, Mary was blindfolded before she took her place at the block in Fotheringhay Castle.

The first blow of the sword missed and struck her head and she whispered "Sweet Jesus" before finally her head rolled from her body.

The Executioner held up the head by the hair and said as he did so:

"God save The Queen!"

But the red tresses were a wig and it was seen that Mary Stuart's own hair underneath it was grey and very short.

The second surprise was when her little Skye terrier who had entered that grisly place hidden under his mistress's skirts appeared and refused to leave her side.

Among the most touching episodes in connection with memorial rings is that exhibited in the closing hours of the unfortunate Mary at Fotheringhay Castle, just previous to her execution.

She distributed the jewels that remained to her among her faithful attendants as tokens of her affection and regard.

Among other sad memorials she desired that a sapphire ring, which she took from her finger, might be conveyed as a mark of grateful acknowledgement, to her brave kinsman Lord Claude Hamilton.

It is a large square sapphire of unusual beauty rose-cut in several diamond points, and set in gold enamelled blue in the curious cinque-cento work of that period.

It is said to be in the possession of the Dukes of Hamilton.

MARY QUEEN OF SCOTS

ELIZABETH, EMPRESS OF AUSTRIA

ELIZABETH, EMPRESS OF AUSTRIA
1837-1898

Elizabeth, Empress of Austria was the most beautiful woman of her age, and still one of the outstanding and greatest beauties in the world.

She was also undoubtedly the finest horsewoman there has ever been.

She was the daughter of Maximilian Joseph and his wife Ludovica, the Duke and Duchess of Bavaria.

The Duke was very Bohemian and wandered about the mountains where he was known as 'Duke Max', and was loved by all the ordinary people he met.

He often took with him his small daughter and she enjoyed an untrammelled and free childhood which was very unusual in those days.

The Princess Elizabeth had been born at Christmas at forty-three minutes past ten.

When the Duke arrived back in the early hours of the morning he looked down at the Baby and felt a strange feeling that the child would mean more to him than any of the rest of his family.

"The little Princess has been born with a tooth in her mouth, Your Grace," the Nurse said proudly.

"Like Napoleon!" the Duke murmured absentmindedly. He was still staring at the child.

He chose her names — Elizabeth Amalie Eugenie — but almost from the first he called her 'Sisi'.

She was with him whenever it was possible and it was he, a great lover of horses, who taught her how to ride.

She was sixteen when it was arranged that Franz Joseph, Emperor of Austria should marry her elder sister Hélène.

The husband proposed for Hélène should have been desirable in the eyes of any girl irrespective of his position.

Franz Joseph was handsome, slender, and broad-shouldered. His eyes were a startling magnetic blue, wide apart, and set off with a broad intelligent forehead.

Hélène however was horrified at the idea of having to marry him because she was already in love.

Franz Joseph had an over-bearing and difficult Mother, and it was the Arch-Duchess who had arranged his marriage.

When the Prince arrived they had arranged a grand dinner for him, but at the last moment the Duke realised they were thirteen.

Sisi was therefore told to put on her best dress, and come downstairs from the Schoolroom to make fourteen.

The moment he saw her Franz Joseph fell in love, something he had never done before.

Early next morning the Arch-Duchess was hardly out of bed before her son went into her bedroom.

"Do you know Sisi?" he asked. "She is enchanting!"

"Sisi!" echoed the Arch-Duchess stiffly. "But she is a child."

"I dare say but look at her red hair, her eyes, her charm, her figure! She is delicious!"

"You know nothing about her," the Arch-Duchess said firmly. "You must examine her more closely. You have plenty of time. There is no hurry! No one expects you to become engaged at once."

"No! No! It is better not to take too long over these things!" Franz Joseph cried, and rushed away in the hope of seeing Sisi again.

Finally he got his way, they became engaged and the marriage was arranged.

The Arch-Duchess however, was to be a dark and evil influence over Elizabeth from the time she married.

She put the whole Court against her and she found fault with everything she did. She gradually spoilt the happiness and love between husband and wife.

It was then Elizabeth took to riding to console herself and her exploits on horseback were talked about all over Europe.

As the years went by she was so famous that people

stared at her wherever she went.

However she became so shy she carried a fan whenever she was out riding.

She grew even more beautiful as the years passed and her red hair adorned with a multitude of diamond stars made every man's heart beat faster the moment he saw her.

She had a sad, and at the end, lonely life.

At the same time many men gave her their hearts and even their lives.

She came to England and Ireland to hunt, and her memory still lingers in the hunting fields of both countries.

As the years passed she was only happy when she was in Hungary where they adored her, and where she had a very romantic relationship.

Finally when she was staying in Lausanne she was assassinated by one of the anarchists as she walked onto a boat on which she was taking a cruise on the lake.

He plunged his stiletto into her breast.

Slowly without uttering a sound, Elizabeth fell backwards onto the ground.

She had asked to be buried in Corfu near the shore and the sea where the waves could dash over her grave.

She had written it in her Will, but like all her deepest wishes in her life this was ignored.

It was Elizabeth's beloved Hungary who had always understood, and made amends the only way they could when their Government obtained permission for the women of the country to subscribe for a monument to be erected near her tomb.

It represents a *Mater Dolorosa*. On Her head is a Crown of Thorns.

ACKNOWLEDGEMENTS

Barbara Cartland wishes to thank the following people very much:

Montgomery Hyde, "The Empress Catherine and Prince Dashkov"; Aubrey Richardson, "The Lover of Queen Elizabeth"; Gina Kaus, "Catherine The Great"; Stafan Zweig, "The Queen of Scots"; Eva Scott, "Six Stuart Sovereigns 1512-1701"; Lt.-Col. Andrew C. P. Haggard, "Sidelights on the Court of France"; Count D'Ornano, "Life and Loves of Marie Walewska"; Barbara Cartland, "Book of Beauty and Health"; Sir Herbert Maxwell, "Sixty Years a Queen"; H. K. Prescot, "The Early and Middle Ages"; Edmund d'Auvergne, "A Queen at Bay"; Martin Hume, "The Wives of Henry VIII"; The Illustrated London News 1900 and 1902"; Neville Connell, "Anne"; Octave Aubry, "Eugenie Empress of France"; Baring Gould, "The Tragedy of The Caesars"; P. W. Sergeant, "The Empress Josephine"; Barbara Cartland, "The Outrageous Queen"; Stenton, "William The Conqueror"; Curties, "A Forgotten Prince of Wales"; Fletcher and Kipling, "A History of England"; Choiseul Gouffier, "Alexander I and Court of Russia"; Charles Petrie, "Louis XIV"; Dunn Paterson, "The Black Prince Edward"; Waliszewski, "Ivan The Terrible"; Cornelius Gurhitt, "August de Starke"; Maura Camazo, "Carlos II Su Corte"; Benjamin Ide Wheeler, "Alexander The Great"; G. F. Kunz, "The Book of The Pearl"; Princess Catherine Radziwill, "Sovereigns & Statesmen of Europe"; Lt.-Col. Andrew Haggard, "The Real Louis XV"; Rachel Challice, "Secret History of The Court of Spain"; Michael Senior, "Richard II"; Francoise de Bernardy, "The Princes of Monaco"; C. C. Trench, "The Royal Malady"; Harmsworth Encyclopaedia, Vol. VI; M. W. Freer, "Henry III of France and Poland"; Alfred E. T. Watson, "King Edward VII as a Sportsman"; Barbara Cartland, "The Fragrant Flower"; Hugh Stokes, "A Prince of

Pleasure Philip of France and His Court"; Michael Prawdin, "The Mad Queen of Spain"; Mrs. Bearne, "A Sister of Marie Antoinette"; Graham, "Life of Alexander II"; Jerome Dreifuss, "The Romances of Catherine and Potemkin"; Francis Cribble, "The Royal House of Portugal"; H.R.H. Prince Tomislav of Yugoslavia; Dr. Rappoport, "Leopold II King of The Belgians"; A. Hilliard Atteridge, "Napoleon's Brothers"; Wilson, "Napoleon The Man"; Frederick de Reichenberg, "Prince Metternich in Love and War"; Barbara Cartland, "The Passionate Diplomat"; Barbara Cartland, "Romantic Royal Marriages"; Edward Legge, "King Edward in His True Colours"; Barbara Cartland, "Diane de Poittiers"; "The Coronation of Their Majesties King George VI and Queen Elizabeth"; "King Alberts Book"; Sigmund Munz, "King Edward VII at Marienbad"; Walter Jerrold, "Henry VIII and His Wives"; Iain Moncreiffe and Don Pottinger, "Simple Heraldry"; Prince Michael of Greece, "Crown Jewels of Britain and Europe"; Guido Gregorietti, "Jewellery Through The Ages"; S. Baring Gould, M.A., "Farouk of Egypt"; David Randall, "Royal Follies"; Daniel George, "A Book of Characters"; Jean Plaidy, "The Spanish Inquisition"; Joanna Richardson, "La Vie Parisienne"; Anita Leslie, "Edwardians in Love"; Barbara Cartland, "The Outrageous Queen'; Barbara Cartland, "Empress of Austria"; Barbara Cartland, "A Year of Royal Days"; Virginia Cowles, "The Romanovs"; Lesley Blanch, "Wilder Shores of Love"; Barbara Cartland, "Love and Lovers"; Barbara Cartland, "Written With Love"; Nina Epton, "Lovers and the French"; Nina Epton, "Lovers and the English"; E. Barrington, "The Laughing Queen"; Beatrice Clay, "Stories of Arthur and The Round Table"; Joanna Richardson, "The Courtesans"; Nancy Mitford, "The Sun King"; G. F. Kunz, "Curious Law of Precious Stones"; G. F. Kunz, "Magic of Jewels and Charms"; William Jones, "Finger Ring Lore"; Thomas Secome, "Twelve Bad Men";

Dorothy Marshall, "Victoria"; Norah Lofts, "Anne Boleyn"; Arthur Vincent, "Twelve Bad Women"; E. F. Benson, "The Kaiser and English Relations"; Longworth, "The Three Empresses"; Erskin, "29 Years of Alfonso XIII of Spain"; Segur, "Marie Antoinette"; Haslip, "Marie Antoinette"; Asprey, "Frederick The Great"; Michael Prestwick, "Edward I"; John Gillingham, "Life and Times of Richard I"; Michael Senior, "Life and Times of Richard II"; Rossabi Khubilia Khan, "Khubilia Khan"; W. B. Henderson, "Life of The Emperor Nero"; Wiegall, "Nero"; R. Davey, "Sultan and His Subjects"; Cronholm, "History of Sweden"; J. S. Orvis, "A Brief History of Poland"; Joan Evans, "Magical Jewels of the Middle Ages and the Renaissance"; Antonia Fraser, "The Kings and Queens of England"; Leslie Field, "The Queens Jewels"; Maurice Ashley, "The Life and Times of King John"; Princess Michael of Kent, "Crowned in a Far Country"; Nancy Mitford, "Frederick The Great"; Suzy Jerkes, "The Royal Jewels"; Alexander von Solodkoff, "Masterpieces from The House of Fabergé; John Lord, "The Maharajas"; Lesley Blanch, "Pavilions of The Heart"; Theo Lang, "My Darling Daisy"; Cecil Woodham Smith, "Queen Victoria"; Elizabeth Longford, "Victoria I"; Antonia Fraser, "Mary Queen of Scots"; Debretts Kings and Queens of Europe; David Williamson, Webb & Bower (Michael Joseph).

OTHER TITLES CURRENTLY AVAILABLE IN

The Royal Series

ROYAL LOVERS

ROYAL ECCENTRICS

Look out for more titles
in this exciting new series in your
bookshop soon